RAPE in America

ISBN-13: 978-1500816520

ISBN-10: 1500816523

RAPE in America

Table of Contents

Chapter 1 – The evolution of men

The evolution of mammals clearly shows a history of male dominance over females, except in the case of a few species such as hyenas. Lionesses will travel with their young and hide them from rogue male rapists if there isn't a strong male to protect them. The evolution of primates also indicates that male hierarchical societies predominate over egalitarian ones, as illustrated by female chimps who will hide their young males from marauding male rapists who will kill them in order to mate with the mothers.

The evolution of humans from the supposed missing link to apes has shown ever more hostile and violent males who rape and kill women. Why? It may on the surface appear as simple as "because they can." However, when we address this pervasive cruel inhumanity to females throughout the history of human beings, the phenomenon of male aggressiveness, rape and murder very complex, multi-dimensional and far reaching.

Men have been raping and killing women throughout history

Chapter 2 – It's in their genes

Men appear to possess an instinctive procreative drive to mate with females (discounting the relatively few who desire to mate with others of their own sex). This appears to be a direct outcome of natural selection, where men who successfully mate with females insure their lineage survives, not that having families and propagating the family surname was much of a consideration prior to the development of complex cultures with distinct social norms and values.

A genetic predisposition for men to rape and kill was a direct consequence of natural selection, where the male progeny of violent rapists and murderers thrived as compared those men with weaker non-violent gene pools, who succumbed to larger more aggressive men and eventually perished or whose numbers decreased into obscurity.

Historically, to the conquerors, go the spoils and women

As human cultures evolved, early human societies gave men certain rights over their women through social norms, and it wasn't but a generation ago when American wives were expected to allow their husbands to pleasure themselves on demand… it was a spousal *duty!* Nor could a wife testify against a husband in a court of law. Not until this current generation has spousal rape become a recognized crime. And in much of the world, females still suffer the inequities and injustices that permit men to rape with impunity. This behavioral expression of the genetic propensity of men to rape and kill women is marginalized and tolerated in certain male chauvinistic societies around the world.

We know through scientific studies that testosterone Is a hormone found in various concentrations in men that stimulate aggressive behavior and sexual arousal. The higher occurrence of testosterone in men versus women (who have higher concentrations of estrogen) appears to be a distinct contributor to violent behavior in men. No wonder the age group of men most likely to indulge in violence, rape and murders are during the period of highest testosterone production in men, because it stimulates and drives men to exact out their natural unchecked urges.

There are males who may be born to be rapists or killers. There are many people born with various forms of mental illness. What we find is the environment of culture, society, personal relationships and various social control or triggering mechanisms have more to do with restraining or releasing the genetic urge that some men have to rape and kill.

SERIAL KILLER'S CRIME DOSSIER

- Feb 1998 Rapes, murders Jayashree
- Nov 1996 Attempts to rape a girl at KEB Colony, Chitradurga
- Nov 1996 Rapes, murders Roopa at KEB Colony, Chitradurga
- March 1997 Escapes from Bellary jail
- July 1997 Arrested; escapes within 24 hours
- Oct 1998 Arrested; escapes again
- In Bangalore Cases in Peenya police station limits, including one of rape and murder
- Faces 21 criminal cases, acquitted in 11, remaining related to rape, murder and robbery
- Involved in cases in Mysore, Mumbai, Ahmedabad and Baroda
- Rapes three girls in Davanagere, Hubli-Dharwad and Pune
- Rapes the daughter of a CRPF commandant and escapes from Kashmir

Chapter 3 - Cultural tolerance

Cultural tradition that turns a blind eye to male chauvinism by assigning specific values to sexual behavior (that it's normal and okay for men, but not for women) has been historically prevalent throughout the world... even to modern times particularly in developing and Third World nations. A man who has sex with many women is usually admired as being virile and a "ladies man", or even "a woman killer"... and sometimes they do just that, follow rape by murder. On the other hand, a female who has multiple male sex partners is decried, ostracized and labeled a whore or harlot, a slut, prostitute and home wrecker. These negative terms are never used in describing men who enjoy having sex with many women, but instead they are minor celebrities for doing it. Women who are "loose" must wear the scarlet letter "H" for being a "Hoe."

Social norms are the direct expression of cultural values. Cultural values and rituals can be compared to the hardwiring of a computer, or the genetic code of specific groups that drives, justifies and perpetuates. Social norms are compared to the phenotypic expression of genetic traits. When culture creates a hierarchical male dominant structure and values, then social norms are the blueprint by which male dominance is implemented, reinforced and executed. In cultures where males rule the coop without question as in Taliban societies, an assassination attempt against a teen age girl for espousing the importance of providing education to other girls is justified and applauded as a social norm, even as their interpretation of male significant religious beliefs do not actually state it. While the western world decried the assassination attempt on Malala's life, most Muslims remained mute. In fact, the feminine agenda is viewed as a destructive aspect of western cultural imperialism by most Islamic people to the point where the majority of Muslim women would agree perhaps the little girl went too far by her impassioned stand on equal rights for educating girls.

Political tolerance of male behavior is typical of most nations because they comprise the vast majority of the ruling parties, whether elected or imposed autocratically. Of the 200 or so formally recognized nations in the world, only 19 or less than 10 percent are women, while females comprise about the same proportion of the human race (a ratio of 101 males to 100 females). Under representation of issues that are important to females result in political blindness and tolerance of male dominant behaviors that often is detrimental to females. While a majority of nations punish rapists and murderers, still many do not. Outside of westernized nations who have accepted the feminist agenda of equal rights for females, the vast majority do not deal harsh punishment for men who rape, or even those who kill women to preserve their personal male ego and family honor.

Religion has been used to rationalize almost all devious behaviors throughout the history of human civilizations. Mass murder in the name of whatever religion has left its horrific mark on mankind. The Nazis who attempted to exterminate all European Jews called themselves Christian and the iron cross came to symbolize their mandate from God to kill Jews.

The Khmer Rouge in Cambodia claimed to be Buddhists who murdered upwards of 3 million of their own innocent people. The Kings of England sent their knights and armies on nine crusades against the Arab world in the name of God. American soldiers were sent to chase down, kill and drive into reservation all of the native inhabitants of what is now the United States of America, because it was "the white man's burden" to civilize savages as a mandate from their Christian God. In every case, the raping, pillage, plunder and mass murder done in the name of religion was committed exclusively by men against innocent weaker men, women, children and the elderly.

The history of modern warfare is no better, just more recent. In all wars, soldiers in battle often raped, tortured and killed innocent females whether they were children or adults. The Japanese did it to the Chinese in WW2. The Americans did it to the Vietnamese during the Vietnam War. And so on. They were rarely if ever punished. Only in the most recent times has the rape and killing of women no longer being recognized as collateral war damage, yet few men guilty of these atrocities are ever punished. No wonder tens of thousands of rapes of women soldiers within the U.S. military is not reported, and when it is, the usually punishment has been a scarlet letter "B" in the files of the women whistle blowers... that being a "cock sucking Bitch." And in Dubai, a Swedish woman was imprisoned after getting drunk and being raped by some Arab men, after she blew the whistle and filed a complaint with the authorities. She was labeled a whore and for breaking Muslim laws that favor the behavior of men and their sexuality rights.

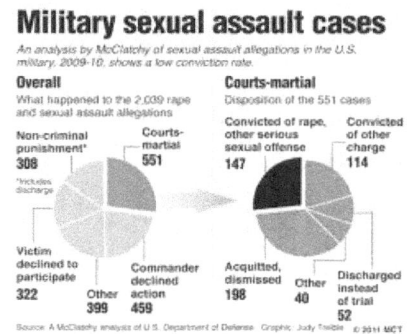

Military sexual assault cases

An analysis by McClatchy of sexual assault allegations in the U.S. military, 2009-10, shows a low conviction rate.

Overall
What happened to the 2,039 rape and sexual assault allegations

Non-criminal punishment*
308
*includes Discharge

Courts-martial
551

Victim declined to participate
322

Other
399

Commander declined action
459

Courts-martial
Disposition of the 551 cases

Convicted of rape, other serious sexual offense
147

Convicted of other charge
114

Acquitted, dismissed
198

Other
40

Discharged instead of trial
52

Source: A McClatchy analysis of U.S. Department of Defense. Graphic: Judy Treible © 2011 MCT

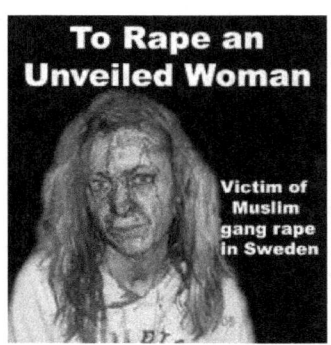

To Rape an Unveiled Woman

Victim of Muslim gang rape in Sweden

Chapter 4 – Childhood issues

Childhood experiences contribute far more to the sexual development of boys and girls than parents and societies would like to admit. Most responsible parents want to shield their children from sexual situations, information or even from exploring their own childhood sexual urges and instinct. Sex in any form is considered inappropriate for children, who should spend their time playing with toys. When sexually explicit dolls like Barbie cause girls to ask potentially sexual questions, parents typically lie to them and invent answers that don't make sense, even to children.

Boys tend to be driven by social norms and genetic propensity to seek active and violent games and toys… pretend guns, violent video games, rough sports and the like. While girls are dressing Barbie, boys are shooting realistic virtual depictions of human beings, when not pretend killing other boys. So how does becoming socially conditioned to kill other males result in boys developing into grown men who rape and kill females?

Statistics indicate that in America, men commit roughly 90 percent of all murders, over 90 percent of all murders by guns, and are killed 3 times more often than females. Yet the preponderance of women killed are killed by men and not by other women. Are men born killers, or does childhood experiences and development greatly contribute to a masculine agenda that includes killing as a right of passage from boy to men?

Childhood trauma also explains how boys react to social situations such as bullying, divorce of parents, child abuse (verbal, physical and sexual) and other negative emotional experiences by developing into aggressive hateful dominating men. Take for instance a boy whose small physical stature or difference in race subjected him to intolerable bullying, ridicule and abuse for many years or his entire childhood when he is developing his attitude toward people in general. Even without interjecting the role of poverty in breeding violent men, this once innocent boy grows up into a man, with a strong virile body filled with hatred for those people who symbolized his oppression. He is wary of other men and buys guns with the intent to use them to prevent ever being violated and attacked ever again. He becomes a ticking time bomb, just waiting for a trigger.

We can't discount the importance of role models in the lives of children, for better or for worse. Successful people tend to come from successful families. Drug addicts and criminals tend to be the result of having parents who deal drugs and commit crimes. Why? It's because their role models become their normal. While there are exceptions, in general the children of wealthy parents who are raised in privileged environments come to take their type of materialistic lifestyles for granted because that's all they know. On the other hand, children who have had to endure poverty and violence express anger and the desire to strike back, or to victimize others as they had been victimized.

Girl siblings in family, and their birth position prior to and after the boys have something to do with the attitudes toward females that boys develop. Sure, most boys go through a stage where they don't like girls because girls are naturally and culturally not Interested in doing the "cool things" that boys rather do. Boys are naturally more "rough and tumble" while girls are more passive. The girls who get involved with sports and prefer to do "boy things" and hang out with the guys are labeled "Tomboys." How boys interact with girls, their female siblings and mothers have some impact on their adult attitudes toward females. Depending on the type and quality of interactions, boys could develop a subconscious disdain for females, or they could feel dependent on feminine nurturance, or many shades in between. Some grow up to become super jealous who feel compelled to physically and sexually abuse women.

Statistics indicate that almost 20 percent of women have been the victims of rape or sexual assault, with almost 18 million being actually raped or attempted to be raped by men. One third of women admit to being in abusive relationships with their men and three fourths personally know another woman who remains in an abusive relationship with a man or who has been raped. This indicates that as boys turn into men, something about their childhood relationships with females just didn't turn out well, and as adults, they find themselves driven by unresolved childhood issues that often manifests as rape and violence toward females, and unfortunately in murder of innocent women whether resulting from jealousy or as easy targets for predatory robberies, rapes and murders. There is currently a manhunt for a guy who killed his friend's estranged wife and son, and kidnapped their 16-year-old daughter. The statistical outcome of such incidents is usually dire, ending with the rape and murder of the female kidnap victim. This follows the conviction of Ariel Castro, a man who held 3 females in bondage over a decade for his own sexual pleasures.

Chapter 5 - Socialization

While children are born with different genetic behavioral propensities, it is predominantly their social experiences as defined by social norms that eventually modes them into the adults who they become. Mass media depictions of sexuality, violence and murder play a large part in how children, boys in particular internalize that information, whether factual or fantasy into their future realities. Consequently, a stimulus is one aspect of the cause and effect equation, and our children are conditioned to have specific attitudes and unconscious automatic behaviors and desires.

The result of the constant bombardment of mass media television, Internet and video games on the developing minds of our youth, particularly boys who spend ten times more effort indulging in violent fantasies than girls, can't be a good thing. The proof is right there on the Internet, in blogs, tweets and comments left by web surfers… of which a casual estimate shows one-third engage in hateful speech, up to the expression of actual specific death threats with details. It is very easy to track down anyone's address on the Internet, and some of these threats of rape, violence and murder are eventually carried out, almost always by men.

Social experiences and interaction by males throughout childhood and subsequent adulthood colors their attitude toward people and they develop a different view on men versus women. Generally, men's social expectation and self-image need is for respect, while women seek love, comfort and security. Tell most men they will be paid $100,000 per year to be treated as a slave,
to be berated, belittled, ridiculed, criticized and offended in public, and the vast majority of men would turn down that job offer without hesitation. Why? Because it does not offer respect. Women on the other hand accept those types of positions without recognizing that once the honeymoon is over, that's called marriage where abusive husbands do not respect their wives. Our social traditions have become so much ingrained and subconscious that men and women play out certain roles without being conscious they are playing this scripted game called gender roles.

The lack of religious indoctrination also removes the restraints from the thoughts of rape, violence and murder. Almost all institutionalized religions and most spin off sects and cults also teach its members various forms of a moral code of behavior. Universal to almost all religions are the values of charity, non-violence, forgiveness and defending the helpless. Those men who have not had a religious foundation in their attitudes and perspectives must rely on the school system, parents, media and self-education through personal experiences for them to develop a personal sense of morality. Many who do not receive religious instruction at key points in their lives are more prone to violence, predatory behaviors, rape and murder… because they may not think there's anything wrong with opportunistic immoral behavior. Unfortunately, many schooled in religious thoughts become hypocrites, including some men of the cloth who molest and rape children. Again, it's the men who are the perpetrators as there are no instances of nuns raping and killing choirboys. So, even religion may not be sufficient to overcome genetic urges, cultural and social norms and dysfunctional childhood experiences.

NAMED AND SHAMED: CATALOGUE OF ABUSE

 Fr Patrick Maguire is believed to have abused hundreds of children in Ireland, the UK and Japan, where he spent 13 years as a missionary. He was jailed for 18 months for child abuse in 1998 and received a six-year sentence in Ireland in 2000 and a three year suspended sentence in 2007.

 Fr Ivan Payne, who was a chaplain at Our Lady's Children's Hospital, is believed to have abused dozens of children. He was convicted of sexually abusing eight boys in 1998. He spent four and a half years in jail. He now lives in Wales.

Fr Harry Moore forced a 16-year-old boy to repeatedly have sex with him between

 July 1984 and March 1985. He was convicted in May 2005 receiving a seven-year suspended sentence.

Fr James McNamee abused more than 20 children in various parishes before being moved on. He has since died.

 Fr Noel Reynolds admitted abusing more than 100 children in eight parishes in the Dublin Archdiocese. He died in 2002.

Fr William Carney abused children between 1974 and 1992. He pleaded guilty to two counts of indecent assault in 1983.

Fr Dominic Savio Boland, 89, was convicted of indecent assault in 2001 and received a

suspended sentence. Lives in a Capuchin Franciscan Order house with restrictions on his activities and ministry.

 Fr Thomas Naughton got three years for abusing four boys in 1998. He pleaded guilty to a new complaint in July and will be sentenced next month.

Fr Donal Gallagher abused at least 14 children. He abused them in confession and washed his hands in the altar bowl. He died in 1994.

Fr John Kinsella was jailed for abusing two boys but released in 2001. His whereabouts are unknown.

Fr Francis McCarthy pleaded guilty to sexually assaulting two young boys in July 1997. He was grated laicisation in 2005.

Chapter 6 - <u>Emotional instability</u>

Sexuality issues generally are deep rooted and complex, and when confronted by men with various personal, emotional and hormonal issues, it is rarely dealt with in honest and factual ways. Most men address their sexuality by rating their personal functionality, size of their genitalia and sexual performance against perceived social norms, whether they are factual or cultural constructions through mass media and peer standards. How they personally rate themselves, as reinforced by their sexual experience with females and comparison to claims by their male associates determine in large part how men perceive their male virility and "macho" manhood rating.

What are the socially constructed benchmarks for sexuality against which both males and females rate men?

- Ability of penis to become fully erect when in intimate contact with women, with or without stimulation
- Minimal average erection size of at least six inches, with seven the preferred length. A flaccid penis should be at least 3 and half inches. The width standard is an inch and half fully erect, and anything less is too thin. A manly stud would certainly exceed these minimal averages.

- Ability to sustain an erection while performing inside a woman's vagina of at least half an hour, not counting foreplay. Anything less is considered premature and selfish. A manly stud would have sexual stamina of at least an hour, and the ability to become erect again to perform within five minutes of ejaculation.

While there have not been authoritative scientific studies of male sexuality that address these factors, these are the primary sexual concerns of most men and consumes their feelings of confidence or inadequacy depending on which part of "average" they perceive themselves. Of course, there have never been studies that attempt to correlate genital size with rape and it appears rapists come in all shapes, sizes and motivations. Some rapists rape for long periods, while many are so aroused that they climax soon after penetration. The part that social norms play in whether men will rape can often be traced to their sexual inadequacy, thus inability to form normal relationships with women who would judge their sexuality and performance poorly. Instead, they might find it more gratifying and empowering to rape without regards to a sexual critique whether by their own perception or by a consenting female. At the minimum, these types of inadequate rapists could feel manly and powerful in overpowering and raping weaker females.

The formation of an inadequate self image from puberty into adulthood defines men's preoccupation with genital size, their physical attractiveness to the opposite sex, confidence level to approach and interact with women, and their level of honesty or delusional rationalizations they may feel necessary to maintain self respect. When the social feedback to their physical aspects exceeds their capabilities, these men feel inadequate with few easy options to improve their lot.

Women can wear make up, have breast implants and wear sexy clothes. Penile implants are rare and often ineffective and could lead to impotence and the costs far exceed that spent by women for highly popular breast enlargements. Men have fewer alternatives that increase their actual sexual value to women. Going to the gym and exercising for hours may make a man fit, but it doesn't make him taller, or his penis any larger, longer and thicker, and may or may not delay his sexual ejaculation one bit. Women can fake orgasms but men cannot because the proof is quite evident.

Inadequate emotional control often leads to men taking the course of violence and rape. This lack of emotional control is often due to a lack of self-acceptance and personally perceived self-worth in the eyes of women. Consequently, they become opportunistic due to weak self-control mechanisms that lead to impatience when they feel sexually over-stimulation due to actual sexual urges reinforced by obsessive fantasies of having sex with women. When their physical sexual urge driven both by hormone and fantasy obsession reach a triggering point, their lack of emotional control fails, and they rape. In many cases, they follow rape with murder either in attempting to either escape arrest and imprisonment, to express deep rooted hatred for women, in an act of anger that they don't have meaningful sexual relationships with women or other unresolved and often unaware undiagnosed psychological and emotional sexual issues.

Jealous rage has often been the motivation for killing women, without prior rape. This violence against women is deeply rooted in social expectations and rules of sexual possession, institutionally defined relationships, and cultural expectations. When men define their masculinity in accordance to dominance and possession of their "love object" that are their girlfriends and wives, they often become enraged when their lover chooses another male as a replacement. Does a woman's choice of another lover make the former male lover less of a man? Subconsciously, yes because the other lover is perceived as a masculinity threat and obviously must be a better lover, otherwise there should be no reason for infidelity, right?

However, the main motivation for jealous rage is just that... unrestrained jealousy that becomes so obsessive and out of control that the enraged male feels compelled to end the pain and torture that he feels emotionally. At that point, grabbing a gun and killing both the ex-lover, her current lover, and then oftentimes committing suicide seems to be the only respectful way out of a situation where he feels he has no more control over. A man who feels he has no control over his life becomes a loose cannon who is capable of destructive and violent behavior, and the triggering mechanism can be as simple as plain old culturally conditioned jealousy that reinforces inherited genetic propensities toward territoriality, male dominance, possession and aggression as part of the evolution of human males.

Sexual perversion has usually been found to be grounded in negative childhood experiences that result in unreasonable and uncontrollable fantasy satisfaction expectations. Perhaps boys who were sexually molested, physically assaulted, emotionally neglected and verbally abused often develop into angry men with sexual dysfunction that can only be satisfied by preying on women. Obviously, they are not able to consistently find willing sexual partners in otherwise healthy relationships, contributing to their desire to rape and molest females.

Deliberate dominance over females is inculcated into boys by cultural and social learning as part of the culture of becoming men. A nice, shy, non-aggressive male is considered a wimp who is not sexually attractive to women who generally desire confident men who take charge. The culture of sexuality also defines for females what types of men are attractive. No wonder so many women fall for the "bad boy" type of guys, feeling special and secure that they have tamed a tough guy who can stand up for himself and be willing to protect her. Unfortunately, too often, it's the bad boys themselves who women need protection from because more often than not, the tough guys have convinced themselves that being tough is acting tough, and dominating women through abusive speech and behavior, including forced sex is the norm, rather than the exception.

Mental illness is the separation of perception from reality and reliance on fantasy and delusion as the basis for perceiving personal reality, decision-making and consequential behaviors. The types of mental illness are wide ranging and often have few curative treatments. Sexual obsession that compels mentally ill men to rape and kill women, such as Charles Manson, occurs in a relatively small percentage of men. Most forms of mental illness more often leads to dysfunctional and inappropriate social speech and behaviors, but can lead to unpredictable violent reactions to real or perceived situations and often what others say is enough to trigger bizarre and aggressive reactions. It is possible those mentally ill men with deficient self-worth could act out anger and sexual fantasies when females trigger their actions from what these deranged men may consider offensive or disrespectful speech. The result could be violence, rape and murder.

Chapter 7- Manhood

Self-image rationalizations occur as self-psychological treatment to overcome self-image deficiencies and to justify reactions to unfair judgment and criticism by others. The mantra is other people are mistreating them, and they must protect themselves from unfair attacks. In this mindset, men can exert unnecessary and unfounded reasons for aggressiveness, and due to a general lack of confidence to confront other aggressive men; they choose to focus on finding justice by punishing the weaker sex. It's always easier and safer to target smaller and weaker people for robbery, rape or murder than to confront a formidable challenge from other men. Women are the preferred victims of choice, particularly for sex crimes. While men kill three times more men than women, killing men is rarely preceded, precipitated or consequential to a sexual assault such as rape.

Men usually kill other men as a result of property crimes such as strong-arm robbery or gang activities related to the drug trade where guns are used in 90% of the killings. In the case of women, violent men who rape are usually motivated by sexual urge, unfettered by social conscience or moral judgment. Some men who become rapists do so because they are unsuccessful at wooing women due to their socially defined unattractiveness… in our society where money and material possessions make men more valuable to women.

Men who cannot accept social reality often rebel against the rules and become opportunistic, predatory, and violent in order to get what they want by force on women that they are not able to get through monetary means.

The socially conditioned attitudes of females toward men who feel unattractive and devalued cause them to believe they are unjustly treated and discriminated against by women. This feeling can justify their aggression against females, up to and leading to rape and sometimes murder. These embittered men often feel that the women they rape actually deserve it as punishment for their imagined wrong doings, and the likelihood that they are whores anyway because they must be having sex with other guys. Predators and sexual crime perpetrators often blame their victims for causing their criminal behaviors due to sexy clothing or showing too much skin that aroused men to rape, particularly if they have consumed excessive amounts of alcohol or are under the influence of certain types of drugs that remove their self control and enable

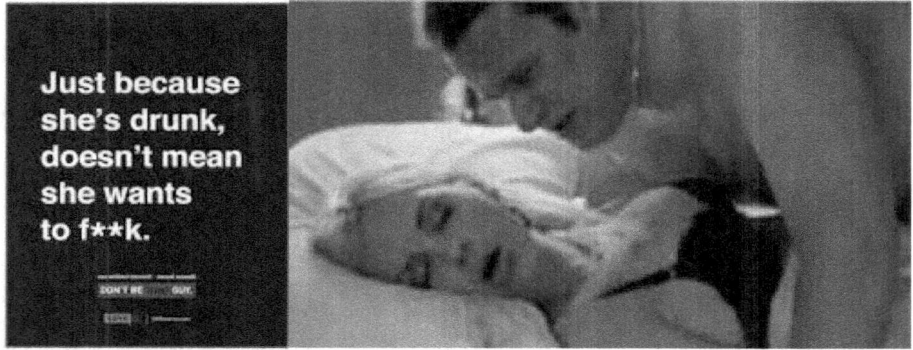

them to act on their urges without restraint.

Chapter 8 - Legal injustices

The ineffectiveness of our legal system to deal with men who rape is clearly evident in a wikipedia article reproduced below:

The U.S. Bureau of Justice Statistics states that 91% of rape victims are female and 9% are male, and 99% of rapists are male.[90] One of six U.S. women has experienced an attempted or completed rape.[91] More than a quarter of college age women report having experienced a rape or rape attempt since age 14.[92] Some types of rape are excluded from official reports altogether (the FBI's definition, for example, used to exclude all rapes except forcible rapes of females), because a significant number of rapes go unreported even when they are included as reportable rapes, and also because a significant number of rapes reported to the police do not advance to prosecution.[93] As well as the large number of rapes that go unreported, only 25% of reported rapes result in arrest.

Many rape kits are not tested.[94] Only 16% of rapes and sexual assaults are reported to the police (Rape in America: A Report to the Nation. 1992 and United Nations Populations Fund, 2000a).[95][96] Factoring in unreported rapes, about 5% of rapists will ever spend a day in jail.[97]

Obviously, with such a low incarceration rate for rapists, it's worth the risk to predatory men who rape and kill. As courts continue to issue mandates for early release of criminals due to prison overcrowding on the grounds of cruel and unusual punishment, it is likely recidivist rapists and sex offenders will be on the prowl. Perhaps the courts need to recognize that there are entirely poor families who share one-room apartments, despite housing zoning regulations, because that's all they can afford. Prisoners already receive free housing, food, health services, and usual protection from other predatory inmates. Perhaps the courts should instead apply those jailhouse standards to hardworking impoverished families who are law abiding and do not rape and kill.

More effective punishments could deter men from raping. Would castration for convicted rapists be considered cruel and unusual punishment? Likely so in a system of justice where men have written almost all of the laws in a culture where the male genitalia is consider so sacristan that a woman who castrated her estranged husband then threw his severed penis into the garbage disposal was given a life sentence for aggravated mayhem and attempted murder. Men who rape women receive an average sentence of between five and seven years, but are can earn early release based on good behavior to alleviate prison overcrowding.

The average sentence for 2nd degree murder in California is 15 years to life, but again subject to parole and early release. The difference between the perpetrators and victims? Women who are raped carry the traumatic memories for a lifetime that could lead to sexual dysfunction and the inability to trust men. If killed, that last forever while the murderer can be released in 8 years.

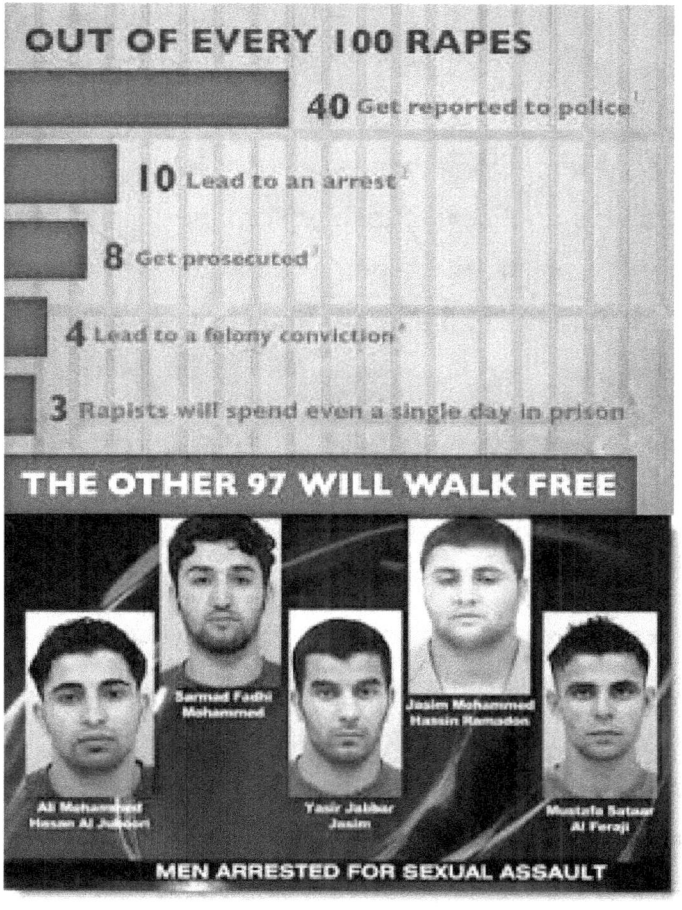

OUT OF EVERY 100 RAPES

40 Get reported to police

10 Lead to an arrest

8 Get prosecuted

4 Lead to a felony conviction

3 Rapists will spend even a single day in prison

THE OTHER 97 WILL WALK FREE

MEN ARRESTED FOR SEXUAL ASSAULT

Chapter 9 – Game changers

What can society at large do to solve this societal illness of rape that almost always targets females? How can women not feed into this paradigm of rape? Some useful advice would be don't tease men because many of them are not able to restrain their sexual urges. Be wary of the men you meet because you don't know their unresolved emotional issues. Don't be alone with men unless there is a high degree of trust that has been earned through respectful and considerate speech and behavior. Don't drink alcohol or take drugs alone with strangers who are likely to take advantage of inebriated or incapacitated women. Rape proof car, home and learn self defense sufficient to fight off a larger and stronger attacker to minimally enable escape, but preferably to disable the attacker.

What can society do to reduce incidences? Education is the fundamental first and most effective step to discourage boys from becoming men who feel rape is okay. This education should begin in the schools, with parental involvement to supplement state mandated sex education classes. Social and cultural values relating to manhood must be examined and corrected where violence and victimization of women is clearly shown to be the likely consequence. Effective medical and psychiatric treatment must be pursued to render rapist incapable of future rapes. This type of treatment should include humane levels of electric shock as part of a comprehensive behavior modification program, supported by appropriate drug and clinical psychiatric therapies.

What can government do that would work? An eye for an eye is justice. Allow the victims of rape to witness the castration of the rapists. This would give retribution and a sense of closure for women who are victims of rape because they would know it can never happen again. Finally, castration of repeat offenders, with a minimum sentence of a decade of incarceration supported by rehabilitation programs, and another decade of electronic monitoring would make the streets safer for girls and women. Repeat rapists must have a GPS computer chip implanted inside them where the sun can't shine.

How can men help other men to control their urges? Rational men need to put other men in check. When other men brag about raping women, instead of joking about it or cajoling the rapists, responsible men should instead report them to the cops. Other men shouldn't feed the egos of braggadocios rapists and must not join in the sexual celebration of disrespecting and dominating unconsenting women. Instead, moral men must take a stand to criticize harshly those men who feel rape is okay, and correct their criminal attitude and behavior and reporting them to police.

Role of parent sets the tone for the emotional development of boys into their pubescence. Parenting must be honest, realistic, protective, communicative and they must set good examples. Abusive men usually develop from abused childhoods. The role of schools is the second leg of developing well-adjusted boys to men. All school instruction and activities should be structured in the framework of equality with mutual respect between the sexes. The greatest culprit for defining sex and gender roles in society fall on mass media whose avarice cause them to exploit sex and sensational celebrity sex scandals. If media programming could instead focus more on the achievements of hard work, charity, inventiveness, creativeness and sacrifice instead of more sex, sex, sex exploitation, rationality could have a chance to prevail.

Media creates sexiness because it sells products, but an unfortunate unintended consequence is rape by disturbed and over immoral sexed men.

Chapter 10 – Gender Roles

Society appears as a matrix of illusions and distortions, as the result of the unequal structure of gender roles and values that prevail in all areas of life and at all levels of human interaction. Why are the basically simple ideas of equality, fairness, and justice so fleeting and unattainable in what we perceive as reality? Is it because we have all been socially, culturally, and philosophically conditioned to suppress our true inner selves in order to conform to an artificially imposed structure of reality that primarily benefits the dominant male status quo? What is the

truer reality that could, would, and should exist were humans permitted and able to shed the suppressive and oppressive veil of social reality based upon gender inequities? Gender disparity is the foundation of the power dichotomy between the sexes that feeds on injustice to the great benefit of men, and at the greater disadvantage and suffering of the world's women. In a gender free egalitarian society, it would be "normal" for people to...

1. Dress anyway they want, for their own comfort and self-expression, without being subjected to ridicule, or social penalties for failing to conform to gender norms;

2. Feel empowered to speak out, to share their feelings and opinions without fear of judgment and ostracism from others for gender-inappropriate views;

3. Have genuine equal opportunity to pursue career, education, association, and lifestyle, without obstruction or intrusion from government and other groups; and,

4. Be liberated from concepts such as masculinity, femininity and sexuaity, and instead respond to their own personal needs and expressions without fear of punishment for non-conformity.

The barriers to the idealistic egalitarian gender-free society are formidable. Gender and sex stereotypes continue to be reinforced and enforced through the social and cultural infrastructure of society. Men continue to maintain a significant advantage in almost all areas of life as compared to women, and gender stereotypes are so pervasive that incremental changes appear to be manifested on a generational level, not as a change to the male power paradigm, but merely as the inclusion of token numbers of females to participate in a power structure designed by men primarily for men. This paper attempts to measure existing gender stereotypes in a college setting, with the presumption that even among higher educated persons, significant traditional sex and gender stereotypes continue to be perceived as the operative reality.

Table I - Survey Methodology and Results

An anonymous sex survey was randomly distributed to both male and female college students at a multi-racial urban university. The sample consisted of 50 females and 50 males. Responses were tabulated and are reported in Appendix B. Any respondent population under 1000 is usually statistically insignificant, and consequently, based on a small sampling of only 100 students, readers should not generalize any trends that the data may appear to suggest.

A. **In general (individual variations aside), which sex does better when compared to the other? Please circle one response for each of the following:**

Average 16 female 34 male 38 both same 8 I'm not sure

B. **In general (individual variations aside), which sex does better in each of the following jobs when compared to the other? Please circle one response for each:**

Female Jobs, Average 51 female 17 male 25 both same 7 Not sure

Male jobs, Average 10 female 64 male 15 both same 11 Not sure

C. **In general (individual variations aside), which sex is a better driver/rider of the following types of vehicles when compared to the other? Please circle one response:**

Average   7 female   60 male   24   both same
9 I'm not sure

D.   Persons of which sex are more likely to have same-sex intimacy (sexual intercourse)?   12 female   17 male   59 both same   12 I'm not sure

E.   The statement, "Size does matter" would best describe the concerns of which sex?   14 females 21 males   31 both same   34 I'm not sure

F.   Which couple do you feel most average people would feel looks odd or weird?   91 short male with tall female   1   short female with tall male
 3 short male with tall male 3   short female with tall female

G.   Body and facial hair looks best on persons of which sex?
0   female   96 male   0   both same   4 I'm not sure

H.   Persons of which sex are more likely to commit violent crimes?
3   female   75 male   9   both same   13 I'm not sure

I.   Regarding your answer in the previous question, do you feel violence is mostly due to: 23   heredity 31 environment   13 culture   30 media

J. Should females be permitted to fight in hand-to-hand combat in the battlefields? 8 yes
62 no 30 I'm not sure

K. Should females be allowed to control the buttons that launches nuclear missiles? 21 yes
37 no 42 I'm not sure

L. Is it the primary role of men in society to protect women?
59 yes 11 no 30 I'm not sure

M. Is it okay for women to wear pants to any type of job, even if it calls for skirts? 52 yes 21
no27 I'm not sure

N. Is it okay for men to wear skirts or dresses in public or in the workplace?
7 yes 66 no 27 I'm not sure

O. In general, would you agree that most women belong to the weaker gender?
59 yes 17 no 24 I'm not sure

P. Would you approve your lover having extra-relational sex if their partner were of the same biological sex? 25 yes 51 no 24 I'm not sure

Q.   If you were born again in the present time, which sex would you want to be?

39 female   47 male   8 both same   6 I'm not sure

The data suggested that many of the male strength, macho, aggression and protection stereotypes remain intact. Females continue to be relegated only secondarily to men, and are generally viewed as the weaker sex, but with more social freedoms than men. Certain gendered social norms are apparent, relating to facial and body hair, clothing options, and perception of violent tendencies. On the measures of career opportunity and options, it appears that respondents recognize that traditionally masculine types of jobs continue to favor men, while women are type cast into lower paying human service jobs where patience is virtue over power.

An unscientific survey of 100 college males and 100 college students was conducted at a California university, with the following gender related questions:

A.   In general (individual variations aside), which sex does better when compared to the other? Please circle one response for each of the following:

1.   Physical strength   a. female   b. male   c. both same   d. I'm not sure

2.   Mental reasoning   a. female   b. male   c. both same   d. I'm not sure

3.   Emotional stability   a. female   b. male   c. both same   d. I'm not sure

4.   Sports performance a. female   b. male   c. both same   d. I'm not sure

5.   Career positions   a. female   b. male   c. both same   d. I'm not sure

6.   Job salaries a. female   b. male   c. both same   d. I'm not sure

7.   Rights, and liberties a. female   b. male   c. both same   d. I'm not sure

8.   Legal protection   a. female   b. male   c. both same   d. I'm not sure

9.   Sexual performance a. female   b. male   c. both same   d. I'm not sure

10.   Independence & power   a. female   b. male   c. both same   d. I'm not sure

B.   In general (individual variations aside), which sex does better in each of the following jobs when compared to the other?   Please circle one response for each:

1.   Firefighter   a. female   b. male   c. both same   d. I'm not sure

2.   Nurse   a. female   b. male   c. both same   d. I'm not sure

3.   Doctor   a. female   b. male   c. both same
d. I'm not sure

4.   Business executive a. female   b. male   c. both
same   d. I'm not sure

5.   Banking executive a. female   b. male   c. both
same   d. I'm not sure

6.   Bank teller   a. female   b. male   c. both same
d. I'm not sure

7.   Preschool Teacher a. female   b. male   c. both
same   d. I'm not sure

8.   Big rig truck driver a. female   b. male   c. both
same   d. I'm not sure

9.   Nurturing parent   a. female   b. male   c. both
same   d. I'm not sure

10. Prostitute   a. female   b. male   c. both
same   d. I'm not sure

11. Military jet pilot   a. female   b. male   c. both
same   d. I'm not sure

**C.   In general (individual variations aside), which sex is
a better driver/rider of the following types of vehicles
when compared to the other? Please circle one response:**

1.   SUVs   a. female   b. male   c. both same
d. I'm not sure

2.   Pick-up trucks   a. female   b. male   c. both
same   d. I'm not sure

3.   Off-road vehicles   a. female   b. male   c. both same   d. I'm not sure

4.   Motorcycles a. female   b. male   c. both same d. I'm not sure

5.   Race cars   a. female   b. male   c. both same   d. I'm not sure

6.   Camper-RV Buses a. female   b. male   c. both same   d. I'm not sure

7.   Speed boat a. female   b. male   c. both same d. I'm not sure

8.   Farm tractor a. female   b. male   c. both same d. I'm not sure

9.   Bulldozer   a. female   b. male   c. both same   d. I'm not sure

10.   Military tank a. female   b. male   c. both same d. I'm not sure

D.   Persons of which sex are more likely to have same-sex intimacy (sexual intercourse)?   a. female   b. male   c. both same   d. I'm not sure

E.   The statement, "Size does matter" would best describe the concerns of which sex? a. females   b. males   c. both same   d. I'm not sure

F.   Which couple do you feel most average people would feel looks odd or weird? a. short male with tall female b. short female with tall male

c. short male with tall female. short female with tall female

G.   Body and facial hair looks best on persons of which sex?

a. female   b. male   c. both same   d. I'm not sure

H.   Persons of which sex are more likely to commit violent crimes?

a. female   b. male   c. both same   d. I'm not sure

I.   Regarding your answer in the previous question, do you feel violence is mostly due to: a. heredity

b. environment   c. culture   d. media

J.   Should females be permitted to fight in hand-to-hand combat in the battlefields?   a. yes   b. no

c. I'm not sure

K.   Should females be allowed to control the buttons that launches nuclear missiles?   a. yes

b. no   c. I'm not sure

L. Is it the primary role of men in society to protect women?

a. yes b. no c. I'm not sure

M. Is it okay for women to wear pants to any type of job, even if it calls for skirts?

a. yes b. no c. I'm not sure

N. Is it okay for men to wear skirts or dresses in public or in the workplace?

a. yes b. no c. I'm not sure

O. In general, would you agree that most women belong to the weaker gender?

a. yes b. no c. I'm not sure

P. Would you approve your lover having extra-relational sex if their partner were of the same biological sex? a. yes b. no c. I'm not sure

Q. If you were born again in the present time, which sex would you want to be?

a. female b. male c. both same d. I'm not sure

Please circle your sex a. female b. male
Your sexual preference a. straight b.. gay
c. lesbian d. "bi" e. none

Please circle your age range   a. 18-24   b. 25-34   c. 35-44   d. 45 and above

Please circle your education   a. HS grad   b. College grad   c. Advanced degree

Table II - Survey Responses

A.   In general (individual variations aside), which sex does better when compared to the other? Please circle one response for each of the following:

1. Physical strength   7 female   72 male   11 both same   10 I'm not sure

2. Mental reasoning   13 female   27 male   53 both same   7 I'm not sure

3. Emotional stability   17 female   21 male   57 both same   5 I'm not sure

4. Sports performance 13 female   46 male   33 both same   8 I'm not sure

5. Career positions   12 female   27 male   45 both same   16 I'm not sure

6. Job salaries   15 female   29 male   41 both same   15 I'm not sure

7. Rights, and liberties 37 female   26 male   38 both same   9 I'm not sure

8.Legal protection   41 female   19 male   35 both same   5 I'm not sure

9.Sexual performance 37 female   26 male   32 both same   5 I'm not sure

10.Public Speaking   16 female   47 male   36 both same   7 I'm not sure

Average   16   34   38   8

B.   In general (individual variations aside), which sex does better in each of the following jobs when compared to the other?   Please circle one response for each:

1.Firefighter   M   5 female   75 male   12 both same   12 Not sure

2.Nurse   F   73 female   13 male   4 both same   4 Not sure

3.Doctor   M   17 female   64 male   6 both same   6 Not sure

4.Corporate Exec   M   13 female   49 male   9 both same   9 Not sure

5.Banking Exec   M 14 female   54 male   10 both same   10 Not sure

6.Bank teller   F 37 female   24 male   5 both same   5 Not sure

7.Preschool Teacher   F 49 female   19 male   5 both same   5 Not sure

8.Big rig truck driver   M 7 female   69 male   3 both same   3 Not sure

9. Nurturing parent	F	37 female	15	male	6	both same	6	Not sure

10.Prostitute	F	44 female	19	male	6	both same	6	Not sure

11. Military Jet Pilot	M	5 female	73	male	5	both same	5	Not sure

12.Cosmetic sales	F	67 female	9	male	14	both same	14	Not sure

**Female Jobs, Average	51 female	17	male	25	both same	7	Not sure**

**Male jobs, Average	10 female	64	male	15	both same	11	Not sure**

**C.	In general (individual variations aside), which sex is a better driver/rider of the following types of vehicles when compared to the other? Please circle one response:**

1.SUVs	16 female	21 male	57 both same	6 I'm not sure

2.Pick-up trucks	11 female	42 male	43 both same	4 I'm not sure

3.Off-road vehicles 7 female	59 male	21 both same 13 I'm not sure

4.Motorcycles	7 female	62 male	19 both same 12 I'm not sure

5.Race cars	5 female	73 male	14 both same 8 I'm not sure

6.Camper-RV Bus   7   female   44   male   26   both same
23   I'm not sure
7.Speed boat   5   female   62   male   21   both same
12   I'm not sure
8.Farm tractor   3   female   72   male   11   both same
14   I'm not sure
9.Bulldozer   3   female   77   male   11   both same
 9   I'm not sure
10.Military tank   4   female   80   male   12   both same
4   I'm not sure

Average   7   60   24   9

D.   Persons of which sex are more likely to have same-sex intimacy (sexual intercourse)?

12   female   17   male   59   both same   12   I'm not sure

E.   The statement, "Size does matter" would best describe the concerns of which sex?   14   females

21   males   31   both same   34   I'm not sure

F.   Which couple do you feel most average people would feel looks odd or weird?   91   short male with

tall female   1   short female with tall male

3   short male with tall male   3   short female with tall female

G.   Body and facial hair looks best on persons of which sex?

0   female   96   male   0   both same   4   I'm not sure

H.   Persons of which sex are more likely to commit violent crimes?
3   female   75   male   9   both same   13   I'm not sure

I.   Regarding your answer in the previous question, do you feel violence is mostly due to: 23   heredity   31   environment   13   culture   30   media

J.   Should females be permitted to fight in hand-to-hand combat in the battlefields?   8   yes   62   no   30   I'm not sure

K.   Should females be allowed to control the buttons that launches nuclear missiles?   21   yes   37   no   42   I'm not sure

L.   Is it the primary role of men in society to protect women?
59   yes   11   no   30   I'm not sure

M.   Is it okay for women to wear pants to any type of job, even if it calls for skirts?   52   yes   21   no   27   I'm not sure

N. **Is it okay for men to wear skirts or dresses in public or in the workplace?**

7   yes   66 no   27   I'm not sure

O. **In general, would you agree that most women belong to the weaker gender?**   59   yes   17 no

24   I'm not sure

P. **Would you approve your lover having extra-relational sex if their partner were of the same biological sex?**   25   yes   51 no 24   I'm not sure

Q. **If you were born again in the present time, which sex would you want to be?**   39   female   47 male   8   both same   6 I'm not sure

Please circle your sex   50   female   50 male
Your sexual preference   88   straight   3 gay
2   lesbian   3   "bi"   4   none

Please circle your age range 71: 18-24   22: 25-34   6: 35-44   1: 45 and above

Please circle your education 76   HS grad   19   College grad   5   Advanced degree

While these results were not statistically significant due to the relatively small sample, the results appear to reflect the general gender stratifications that appear to be perceived by both sexes in society, including alternative sexual orientations.

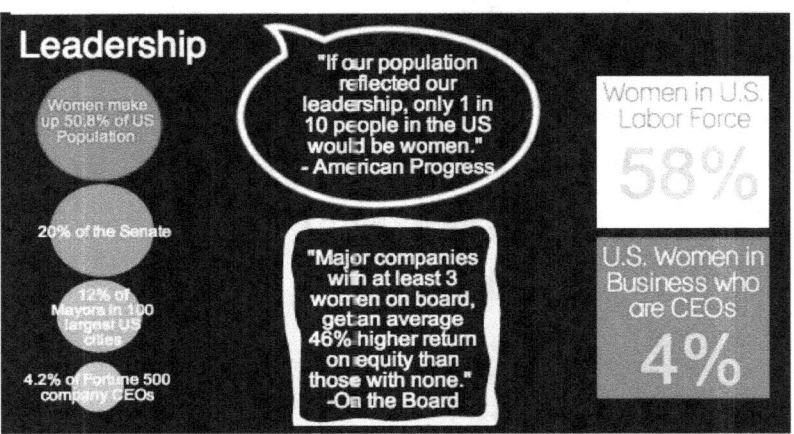

Gender roles begin as fantasies, with outcomes in reality.

Much has been written about gender roles and the divergent social value associated with each sex, leading to the reinforcement of unequal gender roles, expectation, and stereotypes throughout the lives of females. Beginning at birth, parents from high versus low status demonstrate gender preferences that tend to benefit males. Trivers and Willard argue that historically, low-ranking parents have produced the greatest number of grandchildren by investing more in their daughters than their sons, while high-ranking parents achieved the most progeny by investing in sons over daughters. Also, the tendency for parents across all social strata to save more for the college education of their sons than daughters is typical since the expected economic returns are higher for males than for females (Freese & Powell, 1999). Even when women are able to compete "in a man's world", Blair (1999) reports that women have few female role models and believe that their career paths are unpredictable and marked by flukes and accidents.

Furthermore, women face contradictory paradigms for structuring their lives. For example, the male managerial cultural pattern of intense commitment to the organization during the first several years of the career ladder coincides with the life-cycle point at which women are having children. Also in cases where firms disallow married couples to work in the same department, it is generally assumed that the woman rather than her husband would leave due to his typically higher and steadier career path opportunities and income.

―

Even when executive women have prestigious, highly paid jobs, they compare themselves and try to assimilate to the predominantly male management culture, and thus their male dominated financial organizations have been virtually unaffected by feminist concerns (Blair, 1999). Gender inequities show up even at the end of careers, as Han and Moen (1999) observed that gender appears to play an important role in the planning, expectation, and scheduling of retirement, where men are more likely to plan for retirement and to actually retire earlier than women due to the gendered nature of life and career pathways (Han & Moen, 1999).

Gender inequalities "from the cradle to the grave" have been a broad and resistant challenge to the feminist agenda. According to Manza and Brooks (1998), women voters tend to support a wide range of "materialist" social policies such as protective wage and hours laws, expansive health and housing policies, and social provision for homeless women and families, and therefore tend to vote for more expanded social spending by Democrats (Manza & Brooks, 1998). Even so, most men tend to support national defense budget escalations that are usually part of the Republican agenda to reward the military-industrial complex. The hundreds of billions of dollars spent annually on military hardware, international policing functions, foreign and now domestic battle fronts far exceeds that spent on issues that concern feminist causes, besides education.

Meanwhile, mass media continues its daily blitz by depicting females in traditional gender roles, objectifying them for commercial exploitation, and victimizing them as program entertainment. Even where heroines have starring roles, they tend to have an entire supporting cast where they find emotional and physical support and comfort. Buffy the Vampire Slayer, and Zena the Warrior Princess are indicative of the new tougher female characters; however, they are not like Superman, and the Gladiator, who were powerful men who fought alone, and stood on their own feet, without the support of others.

Discussion

The foundation of "isms" lie in the dichotomous power relationship between male and females, where males have parlayed superior upper body strength and aggressiveness into the global institutions of sexism, racism, and elitism. Beginning at birth, males by their "birthright" are placed in a superior position to their mothers, sisters, aunts, grandmothers, and eventually their wives. Almost universally, societies and cultures espouse male dominance and the male agenda, as exploiter and oppressor of females. Men become blind to the
basic contradiction that the females who gave them life, affection, guidance, and nurturance are then castigated into lives of submission, exploitation and violence from men. Civilizations record "his" story, as representative of the greatness of male progress, where females and other

disempowered classes receive little or no recognition for their significant contributions and interventions.

The pursuit of masculine values and benefits have created a severe distortion of the potential for world peace and advancement by focusing natural and human resources primarily on military and monetary acquisitions, resulting in wars and plundering. Power and leadership has almost always resided with males (even where a few females have been the heads of states, they occupied such high positions only through the support of the male-controlled military). Consequently, societies and cultures have generally neglected or devalued those traits typically attributed to femininity and feminism, while praising masculine traits and orientation.

A comparison of prescribed masculine values to feminine values exposes the fundamental contradiction and hypocrisy that has become endemic to the world's social order. The male paradigm emphasizes characteristics that are generally valued as worldly strengths, while the female paradigm is viewed as domestic, sensitive, and weak. Masculine strengths and focus are emphasized in the lexicon of maleness, including competitiveness, winning (at any cost), exploration, discovery, decisiveness, conquering, prevailing, defeating, aggression, leading, persisting, resisting, rebelling, power, control, killing, and war. A perspective of weakness, submission, nurturance, emotionality, obedience, insecurity, fear, dependence, confusion, security, and domestication generally undervalues females.

The man's worldview, preoccupation, and reach is viewed as a global orientation, while the woman's perspective is seen as domestic or regional, or less than the broader scope of men. Let's take a closer look at what the male dominance paradigm has brought to our planet, and ask if traditional feminine attributions might have brought more progress and peace to our world. In our "man's world", humans have experienced violence, war, serfdom, colonialism, slavery, torture, rape, genocide, disorder, starvation, the atomic bomb, and other weapons of mass destruction, while the Earth has undergone mass species extinctions and environmental pollution as the direct consequence of the masculine agenda of greed and conquest. In contrast, the female role and contributions have included birth, rebirth, regeneration, nurturance, cleanliness, social order, communication, cooperation, maintenance, education of the young, peace, and security.

Which does our world need more, the outcomes of the male paradigm that almost invariably leads to warfare, or the female paradigm that leads to birth and regeneration? Presuming a majority of men will philosophically ascribe to regeneration in preference to war and mayhem, what is wrong with the world system that blocks humans from attaining peace, security, and regeneration that the female paradigm represents? What prejudices persist that continue to affront and block the humanitarian evolution of the human species?

Or are we to presume that the underlying factor that has steered the course of human events has been men's biochemical brain chemistry responding to heightened levels of testosterone? Why men are consistently more likely to be violent as compared to women is likely an interaction and product of different brain chemistry and socialization that gives men the feeling and expectation of power, and females the feeling of helplessness, fear and victimization.

It is clear that unless fundamental changes are made to the male paradigm, females will continue to suffer the disadvantages of finding definition in comparison to men. As women's socialization emphasizes their attractiveness and value to men, males are also conditioned to project masculine behaviors to other men. There appears to exist three areas where men exert the most effort to validate themselves before other men, and attempt to build a consistent self-image of masculinity. These three primary areas of masculine validation and reinforcement are 1) masculine occupation, 2) masculine dominance over females, and 3) masculine attitude and behavior.

Men need to feel important and valued. Their high ego needs reflect their constant need to overcome deep-rooted insecurities that of needing to appear, feel, and behave differently from females, which continues to be a devalued paradigm in almost all human societies. The pursuit of male role significance and superiority over females causes men to define their self-identity and sense of self-worth according to their occupation, male-typical behaviors, and dominance over women. Primary indicators of being a "winner" and not a "loser" involves a prestigious job title, income level, degree of supervisory authority, professional designation and independence, physical strength, stamina and skills (blue collar paradigm), and admiration or credit for personal achievements.

Contributing to this drive for manhood is the need to downgrade females as a primary socialization strategy to enforce masculine dominance and valuation. In relationships with women, men express the desire of ownership, dominance and control, and view their objectified female counterparts as sex objects whose role is to comfort and serve male desires and needs. Naturally, this male gaze reinforces their role as the protector of their sexual property, women.

Thirdly, the daily reinvention and reiteration of masculine attitudes and behaviors subjects men to a myriad of prescriptions to prove and validate their manhood to their peers, both male and female. Among these are complex processes and expectations that challenge and stress masculinity as requisites to validate masculine self-worth. "Normal" manly attitudes and behavioral expectations include:

1.   Possessive of personal property

2.   Possessive of females

3.   Protective of females and children

4.   Anti-gay and anti-wimp orientation

5.   Objectification of females

6.   High interest in viewing men sports competitions

7.   Sports participation and competent skills

8.   Beer drinking "with the guys"

9.   Minimal amount of occasional drug indulgence

10. Ability and willingness to fight other guys

11. Mentality for aggression, both verbal and physical

12. Interest and competence in "guy things"

13. Ability to withstand pain without crying, "sucking it in"

14. Not crying in public, except in an acceptable situation

15. Desire to take revenge when wronged by others

16. Rebelling and not cooperating with authority

17. Being independent and uncontrollable

18. Risk taking and dangerous behaviors

19. Doing stupid, ridiculous and risky things to impress

20. Clowning around, joking, teasing, and sexual stuff

21. Talking to others about external, non-disclosing issues

22. Insistence on obtaining "respect" from others

23. Owning male symbols, such as manly vehicles

24. Wearing male validating clothing, and not feminine

25. Not giving up, persistence, and winning at all costs

26. Being physically and sexually attractive to females

27. Ability, desire, or willingness to fight and kill others

28. Affinity for destruction, breaking, and blowing things up

29. Exhibiting bravery and courage and not cowardice

30. Possessing sexual stamina with females

Being a "man" is not an easy task. The lengthy list of criteria places enormous pressure on men to "front" their socialized idea of masculinity to other men, and to women who supposedly (and in too many cases) expect the "entire package" of masculine traits and behaviors. If a man were to demonstrate violations of any of the expected manly behavioral traits, then his manhood is put in question by others, which makes him insecure, and consequently causes him to correct his deviation from the masculine norms, in order to validate his self-worth as a man to himself and to the world of men, and to those women who have bought into masculine gender stereotyping. So much needs to be done to free women from male dominance, exploitation, control, and abuse, but in tandem with female liberation will be the freeing of men from the oppressive male paradigm. Consequently, liberating females from their gender roles serves to free men from the culture of manhood, and all the commensurate, unrealistic, and negative attributes that accompany the masculine paradigm.

Men feel validated by feelings from experiences when facing danger and potential death. Even shy boys, who in the course of growing up are bullied, attempt to overcome childhood emasculation by facing danger, fear, ridicule and prejudice. It is not uncommon in certain parts of rough neighborhoods for boys to be stabbed, beat up, robbed at gun point and have to endure many painful incidents of physical and verbal abuse and violence. Yet they usually survive, only to seek peace and freedom away from violent environments.

Fear and victimization causes life-long trauma and that results in deep-rooted anxieties. I can still feel my skin "tingle" when I enter a "bad neighborhood", and I instantly become more "on guard" and aware of my surroundings. I become more observant of people around me, to ascertain their potential threat level. I avoid certain types of streets, alleys, dead ends, and stay on major thoroughfares, take care of business, then leave as soon as possible. I'm not stupid enough to be caught walking down the street in racial and ethnic enclaves in disadvantaged areas where I would stand out from the crowd. I'm not scared, just experienced and cautious. My observations are well grounded in the reality of street life, as teenage offenders who I teach in juvenile detention camp and alternative school settings confirm it on a regular basis. I have a very intimate understanding of violence, and paroled young adults have described the terrible racial conflict that exists behind the walls of state penitentiaries.

Another consequence of post-traumatic stress is to take proactive steps to increase one's confidence, when avoiding dangerous situations fail to bring security. Self-defense strategy is one very positive program to restore or prepare both women, girls and shy boys to feel more self-confident and empowered. Since nice people can't always avoid jerks and predators, and can't talk them down from aggressive posturing, then they must be prepared to fight them with every ounce of strength in their bodies and minds. It would be much better to get beat up or killed after "trying", rather than "crying" and allowing attackers to be unscathed and uninjured. It's better to teach an attacker the life lesson that they also stand a chance of great bodily harm, or even possible death, than to let them feel that they can victimize others with impunity.

Bullies and violent predatory criminals have no respect, except in the face of a formidable counterforce. The bottom line is a mind set, that if someone has to die at a given moment in time, let it be the one who is the evil one, the predatory attacker. Our community and society needs more people who contribute positively to the world, and the world would be better off for each perverted violent predator who vanishes from the face of the earth.

The deliberate and premeditated victimization of females has been "his" story. Being victimized by a male dominated and controlled hierarchical world social order has been "her" story. We urgently need to press onward to remove the "his" from the story. We need to develop a world that tells an honest story, across ethnic, cultural, sex and gender distinctions. Everyone in the world is uniquely complex and rich with experiences, abilities, skills, and feelings, all yearning to be expressed, accepted, and praised.

Unfortunately, the world is a matrix of lies and illusions, as the result of the unequal structure of sex, gender roles and values that prevail in all areas of life and at all levels of human interaction. Why are the basically simple ideas of equality, fairness, and justice so fleeting and unattainable in what we perceive as reality? Is it because we have all been socially, culturally, and philosophically conditioned to suppress our true inner selves in order to conform to an artificially imposed structure of reality that primarily benefits the dominant male status quo?

What is the truer reality that could, would, and should exist were humans permitted and able (if possible) to shed the suppressive and oppressive veil of social reality based upon gender inequities? Gender disparity is the foundation of the power dichotomy between the sexes that feeds on injustice to the great benefit of men at the greater disadvantage and suffering of the world's women.

If sexism and gender dichotomy didn't exist, each human being would be free to pursue their own personal development in ways that benefit themselves, without feeling the desire to subjugate and exploit others. True freedom of expression from every aspect of one's inner directed being would be possible, resulting in a world where people deal with events, and relate to each other in an acceptable manner, founded squarely in a true reality, and not an artificially imposed illusion of reality based upon social hierarchy and exploitation. Why can't we have a world where:

1. People can dress anyway they want, for their own comfort and self-expression, without being subjected to ridicule, or social penalties for failing to conform to fads and social norms?

2. People not feel intimidated to speak out, to share their feelings and opinions without fear of judgment and ostracism from others, where political correctness does not exist as a concept?

3. People have genuine equal opportunity to pursue career, education, association, and lifestyle, without obstruction or intrusion from parents, government and other groups?

4. Each child born has an unalienable right to adequate love, food, shelter, education, safety, and security, and to be liberated from the fear of uncertainty.

5. People are encouraged to help others, to have ample opportunities to learn the arts, music, literature, theatre, and other cultural diversities, and to enrich their lives and the human spirit?

6. Each individual is liberated from concepts such as masculinity, femininity, and sexuality, and instead respond to their own personal needs and expressions without fear of punishment for non-conformity, as long as others are not hurt?

7. The concepts of race, gender, class, correctness, power, hierarchy, and monetary wealth do not exist, but instead each person is viewed and valued as a uniquely gifted, self-empowered and contributing member to the community of *homo sapiens*?

Now, which reality would most people prefer to live in... the current highly structured illusions that we call reality, or the reality that could exist, if people let it happen? How is the educational system and mass media being responsible in helping people to gain meaningful insights and enlightenment? How can our social institutions give food for thought to present optional worldview to the reality that exist, and ones that might be possible under a different world paradigm?

The pursuit of masculine values and benefits have created a severe distortion of the potential for world peace and advancement by focusing natural and human resources primarily on military and monetary acquisitions, resulting in wars and plundering. Power and leadership has almost always resided with males (even where a few females have been the heads of states, they occupied such high positions only through the support of the male-controlled military). Consequently, societies and cultures have generally neglected or devalued those traits typically attributed to femininity and feminism, while praising masculine traits and orientation.

A comparison of prescribed masculine values to feminine values exposes the fundamental contradiction and hypocrisy that has become endemic to the world's social order. The male paradigm emphasizes characteristics that are generally valued as worldly strengths, while the female paradigm is viewed as domestic, sensitive, and weak. Masculine strengths and focus are emphasized in the lexicon of maleness, including competitiveness, winning (at any cost), exploration, discovery, decisiveness, conquering, prevailing, defeating, aggression, leading, persisting, resisting, rebelling, power, control, killing, and war. A perspective of weakness, submission, nurturance, emotionality, obedience, dependence, confusion, security, fear, and domestication generally undervalues females.

The man's worldview, preoccupation, and reach is viewed as a global orientation, while the woman's perspective is seen as domestic or regional, or less than the broader scope of men. Let's take a closer look at what the male dominance paradigm has brought to our planet, and ask if traditional feminine attributions might have brought more progress and peace to our world. In our "man's world", humans have experienced violence, war, serfdom, colonialism, slavery, torture, rape, genocide, disorder, starvation, the atomic bomb, and other weapons of mass destruction, while the Earth has undergone mass species extinctions as the direct consequence of the masculine agenda of greed and conquest. In contrast, the female role and contributions have included birth, rebirth, regeneration, nurturance, cleanliness, social order, communication, cooperation, maintenance, education of the young, peace, and security.

Which does our world need more, the outcomes of the male paradigm that almost invariably leads to warfare, or the female paradigm that leads to birth and regeneration? Presuming a majority of men will philosophically ascribe to regeneration in preference to war and mayhem, what is wrong with the world system that blocks humans from attaining peace, security, and regeneration that the female paradigm represents? What prejudices persist that continue to affront and block the humanitarian evolution of the human species?

Or are we to presume that the underlying factor that has steered the course of human events has been biochemical brain chemistry responding to heightened levels of testosterone?

Almost all women have to go through negative experiences with men sometime during their lives. Meeting men who appear to be fun, normal, and relatively intelligent is no guarantee they may have met the psycho from hell. Borderline psychotics are attracted to open, kind and vulnerable persons who appear to be defenseless victim types. So-called "friends" become unhappily rejected stalkers whose potentially violent tendencies result in two possible futures, death or the penitentiary.

Statistics indicate that ten percent of the general population has the propensity for great violence, and it's the men in this group that poses the greatest danger to the public, especially to women, because they comprise society's typical predators. Of course, there's also the neighbor next door, the co-worker, the family member, the date, all of whom pose even greater danger because a woman's guard would be down around men they think they can trust.

Statistics also indicate that women stand up to a ten-fold increase of assault, rape, or violence from someone who they know than from a stranger, but the terror is greatest when attacked by strangers because familiarity seems to decrease fear, while increasing anger from victims due to the feeling that their trust was violated. Attacks by strangers involve an animalistic level of fear due to surprise and uncertainty.

Why men are 10 times more likely to be violent as compared to women is likely an interaction and product of different brain chemistry and socialization that gives men the feeling and expectation of power, and females the feeling of helplessness, fear and victimization. The foundation of "isms" lie in the dichotomous power relationship between male and females, where males have parlayed superior upper body strength and aggressiveness into the global institutions of sexism, racism, and elitism.

Beginning at birth, males by their "birthright" are placed in a superior position to their mothers, sisters, aunts, grandmothers, and eventually their wives. Almost universally, societies and cultures espouse male dominance and the male agenda, as exploiter and oppressor of females. Men become blind to the basic contradiction that the females who gave them life, affection, guidance, and nurturance are then castigated into lives of submission, exploitation and violence from men. Civilizations record "his" story, as the truthful representative of the greatness of male progress, where females and other disempowered classes receive little or no recognition for their significant contributions and interventions.

Chapter 11 – Self-protection

In order to empower themselves against aggressors, less physically powerful people, especially women, need to learn alternatives to fight victimization in the form of physical, emotional, and mental self-defense:

1. Physical Defense Strategy: A maximum strategy for maximum danger, or paranoia. A lesser continuum as justified by a higher security level of the immediate environment. These steps are suggested to improve a female chances, when alone, to repel an attack by a determined predatory attacker, and to survive. The suggestions are for maximum defense.

a. Learn practical self-defense techniques, both weaponless, and with various weapons that can be readily found in the environment, like a sharp car key, belt, sharp pen, purse strap, pump heels, rocks, forks, spoons, pots and pans, furniture, lamps, fire extinguisher, and whatever is near by during an attack. Basic self-defense includes using an attacker's weight and momentum against him, and using the hard surfaces from one's body (elbow, fist, hand ridge, knees, head, heel, etc.) against the soft surfaces of the attacker (testicles, throat, eyes, ears, etc.). Full contact self defense training is essential to provide a realistic experience in how it feels to strike an attacker with full force.

b.   Carry legal self-defense weapons, like pepper spray or a stun gun, ready for use when in an uncomfortable or potentially foreboding environment. A blinding halogen flashlight is also helpful during nighttime attacks. Be familiar with its use, and never carry a weapon that can be taken away and used for deadly harm against the potential victim.

c.   Learn to use a firearm, knife, pipe, stick, and other objects that can be stored in handy places somewhere in each room, near where women are more likely to spend more time. Depending upon the safety of one's neighborhood, there should be at least one object that can be used as a self-defense weapon in each room of one's house, hidden, and known only to the resident. However, care should be used if there are small or immature minors at home. For example:

        1)   Bedroom door is alarmed, minimally with a trip alarm that sounds a high decibel screech. Objects are strategically tied to curtains and blinds next to windows, which will fall over with great noise if an intruder enters, to supplement an electronic window alarms system. Pepper spray should be placed on the bed stand next to one's clock, safety off, to be reachable. A loaded small caliber gun, cocked and with safety on (and trigger locked if minors reside in home) should be placed beneath the bed, so if attacked, the woman can fall to the floor and have a chance to grab and use the gun (the gun is unlocked and ready for use after retiring to bedroom to sleep). The smaller caliber gun (.22 caliber)

---

may not kill a large male, but gives the woman a chance to get up and run to the place where her larger caliber weapon is ready for use. According to the NRA, at least 200,000 incidents per year of gun-related home defense occur annually, compared to 8,000 homicides on a national basis. There should also be sharp hair pins and letter openers handily on the dresser, near the makeup vanity, and also taped to the bottom of the sitting chair. Bedroom doors and locks should be strong, with key access, to keep out a large charging man.

2) Bathroom: take your loaded gun with you into the shower or bath, but try not to drop it into the soapy water (but it'll still work when wet). The handle of the bathroom plunger should be sharpened (and a metal cross bow arrow tip installed), and covered with a plastic cap that can be easily removed, and used a thrusting weapon to the surprise of any attacker. Toothbrushes can also be sharpened and capped off. Tape a 2-inch knife to the bottom of the sink, and place one in the medicine cabinet, and also placed in the hollow shower curtain tube, and inside towel rack hangers. The bathroom door should be strong, with strong key-accessible deadbolt, and you should have your cell phone handy.

3)   Kitchen: hide and lock all large knives when not being used. Place sharp 2-inch knives (blade length) in several places (in a few pots, in the dirt of a potted plant, under the chopping board, taped to the side of the range, under or on tope of a shelf, etc.). The small knife is enough to cause pain to an attacker, to allow the female to run to the bedroom for the phone and backup firearm. Leaving large knives around enables burglars to arm themselves, and if taken away from the woman, used against her by a stronger upper body man, with a stronger grip and greater aggression.

4)   Living Room and Den: pepper spray taped to the T.V. remote control (placed out of reach if very small children are around, when not being used with T.V.). Older children should be taught how to use it. Small 2 inch blade knives strategically taped to the bottom of tables and chairs where the woman is most likely to be sitting if an intruder was to break in. Everything must be out of the reach of small children, and older children must be warned and taught on its proper use, only during incident of attack, and not on each other. Children who fight should be kept away from any weapons of any type, as they are too unpredictable and may use it against each other.

5)   Garage: a peephole to the garage from the adjoining interior door should provide a view of the entire garage when lit up. A motion detector alarm system should be

armed. Some intruders have access to universal garage openers that can open your garage door. When driving in to the garage, look in the rear view mirror as pulling in, to make sure no one has followed you in. If so, back the car out, and if the intruder is stupid enough to stand behind your car, slowly nudge him out of the way, but don't panic and deliberately run him down... you may kill him. Of course, if he has a gun, duck down, step on the gas, and back the car out quickly to leave the scene. If the gun-toting intruder is hit, then he had it coming. At least you're more likely to escape and live.

6)   At work, universally, all employers ban weapons in the work place. However, women also have the right against illegal search and seizure from their private property, their purses. Pepper spray hooked to your key ring, another in the purse, tough finger nail files, letter openers, an electronic stun gun, and two inch knife would likely be legal. Carry one, or all, depending on a woman's level of anxiety and concern.

7)   Parking lots and parking structures are potentially dangerous places, especially in certain neighborhoods, particularly after dark when fewer people are around, because predators are opportunistic attackers. The key-ring pepper spray and sharp finger nail file can buy time for the female to scream "fire", "help me", which gets more attention than just screaming. If an attacker is able to get a woman into a vehicle, there's a very high

probability she will be raped, tortured, and/or murdered, possibly never to be found again. It is much better for a woman to fall to the ground, and continue to scream and fight, than to cooperate and enter a vehicle. Predators don't want to work all that hard to get a victim, and the more a woman fights in a public area, the less she will have to fight in a remote environment, like an alley, in the forest, desert, or deserted building. It's more likely a predatory attacker will give up and wait for a chance later at a much easier target.

2. There are also incidents where a single predatory attacker is much too big and strong to be hurt by a smaller person. Some men can take a hard kick to the testicles, direct strike to their throat, or a jab to the eyes, and still manage to get their strong hands and body on the intended victim. Ideally, a victim is able to keep sufficient distance between themselves and the attacker to avoid getting grabbed. For example, placing a car between a potential attackers is a prudent strategy, by going to unlock the door that places the car between a potential attacker and victim. Running around the car to avoid capture while screaming will also frustrate and discourage most unarmed attackers. Always keep a large sharpened screwdriver hidden in the car's trunk, and learn how to pop open the trunk if placed inside by an attacker. The "club" also makes a handy striking weapon, but it can be taken away if a person doesn't know how to use it properly in close fighting quarters.

3.   Mental and emotional strategies are as important, or even more important than physical abilities. Multiple attackers, armed predators (with guns or knives) cancel most chances of using self-defense techniques or non-lethal weapons (unless the victim already has a loaded gun, cocked, safety off, trigger lock off, and ready to aim and fire, and the intended victim is a damn good shot, and not afraid or morally against shooting another person in self-defense). A well-trained fighter (like a Navy Seal or Green Beret) stands a 50% chance of coming out alive against 3 or more men armed with guns who are willing to use them, when the trained fighter is unarmed. Any average man or woman's chances are much less to nil in this case. Better to use persuasion at this juncture.

Sometimes, pretending to go along with the attacker's program when they are heavily armed, buys a person time to think of escape strategies. Think escape, not fighting back, or the trigger-happy assailants will most likely shoot the victim. A crazed man with a gun has a very different level of agitation and mind set from those who are not willing to use deadly force. A man with a gun is likely not to have moral questions about shooting someone, if he becomes fearful, excited, agitated, or irritated. Cooperate to buy time, and hope he's a bad shot when the opportunity arises for a quick departure (like jumping out of a moving car going 20 mph or less, but knowing how to fall and roll because hitting the pavement will definitely hurt).

All things being said, being aware of one's environment, listening to one's intuition (and women are known to have a better "sixth sense" than most men), assessing potential danger from the situation and people, keeping open a quick escape route, and using non-lethal armed and non-armed self-defense techniques and weapons when verbal interaction fails, to provide escape is probably an effective strategy to avoid capture, violence, and perhaps death. Use verbal and mental skills to assess and emotionally disarm and calm attackers when captive, and looking for opportunities to buy time to escape is essential if kidnapped, but relatively unharmed. If a woman or man has used all of her/his wit, strength, and self-defense training to escape or incapacitate an attacker, they greatly improve their chance for survival. But nothing in life is guaranteed, so if victims should be killed, at least they go out "fighting for their lives", and not as "road kill".

At times, in the rare situation, that's the best a person can hope for; to be able to deliver a counterforce blow to an evil attacker that puts them out of the business of hurting another person. Maybe the attacker loses an eye to the victim, and at times in life, some people's death serves to prevent many others from dying; which is the case of our brave American fighting forces, both women and men, in many nations around the world. If a person must die, there is no greater honor than having fought one's best fight, in the service of one's loved ones and country, for noble principles such as democracy, freedom, liberty, justice, and the American way of life. In the urban battlefields, each citizen has a responsibility to show courage, and to come to the calling of fellow citizens against evil, as long as the actions taken are proper and allowed under the rule of law and good Samaritans, and are not acts of vigilantism. A potential victim has to do what they gotta do, especially if faced with overpowering danger from predatory males who seek females, the young, and the defenseless as their next victims.

The best defense against potential male predators is prevention and avoidance. It's continues to be true that too many females are attracted to the confident, cocky, physical guys who often turn out to be aggressive and inconsiderate jerks, sometimes jealous and maniacal rapist killers. A rather obvious gender based difference between men and women are attributes assigned to aggressive versus submissive personality types. We all go through life and are forced to deal with people one way or another, whether we want to, need to, like it or not. Generally, as we stumble through our life's path, we tend to meet primarily two types of people to various degrees on the continuum of behavior. This short paper offers an in depth comparison of these two types of personalities, with the hope that readers will recognize the connection between how certain people treat others and their core character.

If you find a person displays half a dozen of these behaviors and attitudes, be aware that it's likely part of the character pattern that makes nice people and mean people polar opposites. It's very difficult for nice people to be mean, and vice versa, mean people can "fake it" and be nice for only a short period before their true character shows itself through their demanding, aggressive, deceptive, manipulative, inconsiderate, insensitive, and mean manner. Let's compare the two types of men that women are likely to find when they weight the decision to settle for a nice guy, or to seek the "bad boy" types. What are the typical differences between unimposing men versus confident types? The significance of this comparison is the fact that nice guys rarely rape, while many bad boys don't think there's anything wrong with dominating women, up to an including rape.

NICE GUYS		BAD BOYS	
1.	Considerate	1.	Inconsiderate
2.	Compassionate	2.	Cold-hearted
3.	Humble	3.	Arrogant
4.	Selfless	4.	Selfish
5.	Cooperative	5.	Dictatorial
6.	Giving and charitable	6.	Demanding/taking
7.	Fearful and anxious	7.	Fearless/aggressive
8.	Innocent	8.	Predatory
9.	Insecure	9.	Over-confident
10.	Under-achiever	10.	Over-achiever

11.	Open-minded	11.	Opinionated
12.	Approval seeking	12.	Credit/ seeking
13.	Guilt complex	13.	Blameless/guiltless
14.	Self-deprecating	14.	Self-righteous
15.	Courteous	15.	Rude
16.	Moralistic	16.	Immoral or amoral
17.	Sacrificing	17.	Opportunistic
18.	Apologetic	18.	Ass kicking
19.	Helpful disposition	19.	Obsessed to win
20.	Kind	20.	Stingy
21.	Honest	21.	Deceptive
22.	Mellow and easy-going	22.	Angry and driven
23.	Patient	23.	Impatient
24.	Accepts blame	24.	Blames others
25.	Supporting	25.	Leading

26. Status quo maintainer vs. competitive or destructive

27. Goes with the flow vs. it's their way or the highway

28. Feels used and unappreciated vs. feels never enough

29. Worries about others vs. worries about self

30. A friend you can trust vs. just another user asshole

31. Ethical conduct vs. unethical

32. Peaceful resolution seeking vs. violence prone

33. Loyal vs. disloyal

34. Open-minded vs. rigid and opinionated

35. Willing to admit mistakes vs. self-righteous

36. Tolerant and accepting of others vs. intolerant/bigoted

37. Sincere vs. manipulative & insincere

38. Trusting vs. distrusting

39. Dependable vs. unreliable

40. Predictable vs. unpredictable

41. Trustworthy vs. takes advantage of trust

42. Creative and supportive maintainer vs. destroyer

43. Forgiving vs. revengeful

44. Loving and kind vs. angry, hateful and miserly

45. Accepting of differences vs. prejudice

46. Sexually considerate vs. promiscuous/aggressive

47. Facts are interpretive vs. facts are absolute

48. Intelligence is developed vs. intelligence is inherited

49. Freedom of choice vs. control is power

50. Good health is internal vs. health is superior strength

51. Money is pragmatic and functional vs. money is control

52. Accepts aging process vs. wants to live forever

53. Being average is acceptable vs. elitist attitudes

54. Wealth is desirable vs. wealth is essential

55. Religious tolerance vs. religious hypocrisy

56. Beauty is only skin deep vs. beauty is a commodity

57. Appropriate for situation vs. whatever, whenever

58. Act legal and appropriate vs. impulsive without guilt

59. Eat to satisfy hunger vs. eat whatever as much as want

60. Sex is expression of love vs. sex is power recreation

61. Do what's affordable vs. do whatever desired

62. Rules should restrain urges vs. rules don't apply

63. Avoid trouble by knowing limits vs. push the limits

64. Seek others to cooperate vs. outsmart and command

—

65. Be humble in achievement vs. win at all cost, then brag
66. Conserve for a rainy day vs. get other people's share
67. Take prudent step everyday vs. gamble on high risks
68. Be fair and reasonable vs. attack and conquer
69. Other's welfare is important vs. no body else matters
70. Plan future and act safely vs. react forcefully, dominate

More differences between nice guys versus bad boys

Observation: Bad boys seek out nice females because they tend to be users, abusers, and predators. They possess a more pronounced hunter instinct that's hereditarily akin to animals. These **alphas** define, drive, and destroy our world, which otherwise would be too nice. Nice guys desire peace, freedom, brotherhood, family, love, civility, human dignity, human rights, and prefer to obey the law. Bad boys want power, control, money, exploitation of others, self-centeredness, materialism, and don't like following society's rules, as they desire to be above the law. Following is a real example that distinguishes nice guys from bad boys:

There are many significant difference between people who prefer by choice to be nice and considerate versus those who often get their way by being mean, demanding, and selfish. Here's a description of a person, whom you may recognize among your associates or family members. This person may appear to be fictional, but the illustration is factual of the heightened tension and drama that personifies many *mean-spirited* people. Oftentimes, nice people may feel the following describes people who are *crazy* or *bi-polar*, but whatever euphemism is used, the actions are similar and fall into the *pattern of bullying usually exhibited by bad boys.*

Description of behavior and attitudes of a bad boys:

1.   Makes decisions impulsively and impatient for gratification.
2.   Insists on self-correctness and doggedly defends position, stubborn.
3.   Changes mind on direction of action depending upon mood and impulse.
4.   Insults people if their views are in opposition, calling others stupid.
5.   Repetitious of certain favorite stories or phrases from their life experience.
6.   Self-indulgence in everything, and highly self-centered.
7.   Sometimes complements, but negates it with ten times more negative criticism.
8.   Blames others if things don't work out their way.
9.   Takes contrary view, or criticizes other's positions, just to find faults.
10.   Expects people to say and do things in the way according to their expectations.
11.   Intolerant of interruptions, as what they say is always more important.

12.   Challenges other people's facts as conjecture and suppositions, while imposing their personal views and perspectives as factual.

13.   Takes a historical view with little futuristic orientation or broad view of the world.

14.   High risk behaviors and risk seeker, looking for action, contest, and competition.

15.   Fearless when having the upper hand.

16.   Revengeful and aggressive.

17.   Obsessive and compulsive.

18.   Triggers to high verbal volatility and aggressive profane barrages.

19.   Disinterested in other's views, which are considered unimportant, stupid, or retarded.

20.   Competitive, if personally affected, and wants to win at all cost.

21.   Racist view of world, interpersonal relations, and social economic order.

22.   Punitive; threat oriented when feeling in charge, control freak.

23.   Resist expressing positive emotions as sign of weakness.

24.   Contradictory morality or immoral.

25.   Rebellious against others who attempt to exercise influence or control.

26.   Leaves fate blowing in the wind and will try anything if in the mood.

27. Doesn't give a damn, even if the worse consequences are possible.

28. Not compassionate, it's other people's own fault for bad things happening.

29. Manipulative, and will befriend if potential benefits in various ways.

30. Disloyal to family and loved ones, and unfaithful to lover; opportunistic.

31. Secretive, tells you what she wants you to know or think, not often the truth.

32. Highly calculating and manipulative of immediate environment.

33. Highly exploitive in diverse and changing situations and opportunities.

34. Realistic and pragmatic view and approach to using people for self gain.

35. Inability to feel guilt, and or to love deeply.

36. Attracted to superficial appearances, people are like candy in a store.

37. Able to withstand high degree of physical pain and punishment to get self-benefits.

38. Feels they are superior and deserve to be a served and kiss-up to by others.

39. Desires total freedom and no commitments to others.

40. Persistent, compulsive, obsessive, extreme, and determined at all cost if necessary.

Ironically, both nice people, as well as mean people are attracted to nice people. Nice people enjoy being around nice people because it's a time for sharing, caring, communications, relaxation and enjoyment. Mean people want to be around nice people in order to be served, to take advantage, boss others around, get nice people to do things they are either too lazy to do, or don't feel like doing. And when mean people don't get their way immediately, they tend to yell, insult, and express rage like spoiled brats who never grew up emotionally. Unfortunately, those who rise to the top of organizations tend to be these mean-spirited and driven ass-holes because they refuse the alternative of going along with others, instead of always getting their own way.

These mean-spirited predators feel no shame or guilt in backstabbing competitors, associates, friends, or family if anyone gets in their way of achieving their compulsive goals. Often, they get so used to others giving in to their demanding manner, that they don't even think they're being inconsiderate or mean. It never crosses their mind that they are the source of conflict and discomfort to others, because most people are willing to let mean people have their way, just to avoid all the unnecessary drama and conflict, usually over stupid and unimportant issues. And even when aggressive people realize they are being jerks, they enjoy the feeling of having power and control over others, making others run around like trained dogs. The feeling of power and invincibility is an aphrodisiac that reinforces mean people's rude behavior, and therefore it would be very foolish of nice people to ever expect mean people to change their stripes because they gain too much benefit from their instinctive predatory behavior.

The best thing nice people can do is to avoid bad boys who are mean people, to deprive them of their predatory ways. If all the nice people could someday band together and force mean people to change their ways, to be more humane and less despicable, the societies in the world would be a much nicer place, where people could become more fulfilled and happy. Unfortunately, it's the mean people who rule the world, own the world's resources, command governments and militaries, and enforce laws that keep them in control of the world's nice and meek people.

The historical world paradigm has not been one of **survival of the fittest**, but instead, **survival of the baddest – the meanest**. And perhaps that paradigm will never change in our lifetime because nice people will always give in to mean people, if for no other reason than to avoid conflict, and have some peace of mind away from dramatic, demanding, and aggressive mean people.

When confronted, mean people will often claim they were not aware how people viewed their behavior as being demanding and mean-spirited. Mean people become accustomed to getting their way by being inconsiderate of the needs of others. By being demanding of others, they get others to do the difficult part of work, while mean people stand around to criticize and give orders, then call that leadership. They will justify their behavior by saying they have high expectations, and want to push people to their highest potential – when in fact, these bosses probably don't have the knowledge and skills to achieve what they expect of others.

It is the typical CEO or "boss" mentality to exploit workers labor, to do things that bosses can't often do themselves. Mean people often feel compelled to push others out of their way, disregarding other's rights and needs, and will attempt to cut in line, even though others have patiently waited for their respective turns. Mean people feel comfortable using others to obtain personal gain, glory, and credit that would otherwise be due to others who actually accomplish the work. Of course when things don't go the way mean people want, they're the first to accuse and blame others for mistakes, wrongdoings, and crimes while
attempting to exonerate their implicit knowledge and responsibility for the outcomes. They jump at the chance to claim credit for any achievement, and hide behind the otherwise good name of an underling who would be sacrificed to protect the bosses against penalties.

Why is the world still a dangerous and violent place? Is it because we have too many nice people? Or is it because mean people create conflict, violence, exploitation and abuse? It takes about 100 really nice people to neutralize one mean person. Now, if you were to count all the nice people you know (hopefully starting with you), versus the mean people, it would be very difficult to name 100 nice people for every mean one that crosses your path. That's too bad, because it dooms humanity to its primal stone age instincts, which prohibits enlightenment and humanitarian progress that is yearned for all over the world. With the coming advent of total economic and political globalization coupled with the rule of despots in developing countries, the future looks rather bleak for the world's majority of nice people.

Undoubtedly, nice people will again become the cannon fodder, and the exploited class of low-wage laborers for the foreseeable future. The only alternative is for nice people to stand up and refuse to do the bidding of mean people, but that's a spiritual revolution that comes with great penalties, pain, and punishment for nice people. And getting embroiled in conflict, violence, and anger does not describe the type of environment

and mindset that fulfills nice people's lives; however, mean people seem to thrive on negativity and conflict. Mean people certainly have a clear advantage in the system of things in human societies and civilizations. And it's unlikely this paradigm will change anytime soon.

Chapter 12 – Civilized Society

The United States of America has become one of the most crime ridden and violent societies in modern times, while Singapore has one of the lowest crime rates in the world. Less than 200 women are raped each year. The murder rate is exceptionally low when compared to other nations. The public administration environment in modern-day Singapore finds its roots in 1960's with the establishment of meritocracy and individual responsibility as the primary foundation of social order and their social-political culture. The political and bureaucratic implementation of caning of American teenager Michael Fay in 1994 for the property crime of vandalism was a analogous microcosm that demonstrates Singapore's high regard for their public administration's important role to ensure social order.

Even while caning was characterized by the American press and Amnesty International as evidence of barbarism, extreme cruelty, and human rights abuse, Singapore's and their political, judicial, and public administration system viewed caning as its sovereign right to determine appropriate domestic expectations in the manner its citizens and others inhabitants within their sovereign state should behave.

Almost a year prior to international criticism that otherwise detracted from Singapore's image of a civilized and orderly society, a People's Action Party (PAP) member of Parliament, Koo Tsai Kee wrote to The Straits Times, elaborating on fundamental philosophical differences between the socio-political values of Singapore and typical Western views. He observed that a tendency exist, especially among nations in the West, to ask society to share as a contributing factor to individuals' crimes, whether it be assault, drug-taking, vandalism, or murder. He further adds, "When individuals commit crimes, society is asked to share the blame. There is no demand for individual accountability. There is no right or wrong. This is misplaced compassion ...We must never let the pseudo-scientific explanations of some social scientists on human behavior confuse us into accepting over-compassion.

Singaporeans must realize that our almost crime-free society has come about partly because we always ask individuals to differentiate between right and wrong and partly because we know that under Singapore's law, persons convicted of crime have to take personal responsibility. Society cannot share his blame. It is the certainty and severity of punishment that have kept Singapore a safe and orderly society." (Perera, pg.2).

Generally, in America and most European nations, cultural values evolve and change, which are reflected in the polity and consequential laws. In Singapore, the bureaucracy sees its primary roles as one to support the efforts of high government officials to influence and set boundaries for the expectation of civilized citizen behavior as defined by t heir conservative moral cultural values and codes. In turn, each individual, especially those bureaucrats whose purpose is to serve the public good, are expected to take on individual responsibility to be meritorious and good examples of moral behavior. To encourage this symbiotic relationship between the bureaucratic state as the protectorate of civilized society, the government system encourages and rewards public servants based upon meritocracy in personnel policies and procedures.

Singapore is an enigma of sorts, being a synthesis of Confucian principles of collectivism, consensus, and hierarchy while adopting Western concepts of individualism and political participation, equal opportunity, the merit system, free market economics, and disciplined social order as induced through state interventionism by the public bureaucracy's implementation of government policies and programs (Simone, pgs. 278-280). The government's ability to promote economic development and social stability and order in a multiethnic society has been possible through the workings of a highly competent and uncorrupted paternalistic bureaucracy, and by manipulating democratic participation by using rewards for submission and punishment for opposition to state authority, while upholding the outward appearance of democracy. An important aspect of Singaporean identity is their society's (government's) ability to provide good health, housing, education and social order in return for accepting restrictions on freedom of speech, the press, assembly, and unionism (Simon, pg. 173).

Singapore's Senior Minister and predominant political official, Lee Kuan Yew responded to news media questioning regarding caning of an American teen, observed "Can we then cane any other foreigner or our own people?... I am an old-style Singaporean who believes that to govern you must have a certain moral authority. If we do not cane him because he is an American, I believe we'll lose our moral authority and our right to govern... little countries protect themselves in a different way. We don't deal with criminal behavior the way Americans do. We don't have the concept of "victim of society".... This concept has led to a situation where if you kill your mother and father, because you were victims, you are not guilty... If we allow it to be O.K., we'll have chaos. Maybe we are old-fashioned, maybe we are reactionary, but the place works... We take a fundamentally different approach. We believe we had to take strong measures to make sure that people understand that other people's lives, their persons and properties have to be respected. we should continue that. The government can set the parameters.... " (Lee & Gaines, et al).

Unique Features are comprehensively described by Wong & Chan (pgs. 1-18, 47), and summarized as follows:

I.   Public Administration in Singapore as a Consequence of Continuity and Reform.

The Singaporean system of government is based upon the Parliamentary or Westminster model where executive power resides in a cabinet that is responsible to and appointed from a unicameral elected parliament in a one-party-dominated system. Under the direction of the cabinet are the public administration institutions that comprise the public face and actions of state, and top civil servants as well as ministers typically sit on the boards of such agencies. In addition, there exists an extensive network of government-linked companies in which the state has a majority or sizable shareholding, and which operate like privately owned companies, having to compete and make profits without financial assistance from the state (pg. 1-2).

II.   Public Administration Paradigms in Singapore.

A.   Meritocracy with recruitment, promotion, and ranking is based upon qualifications, performance and potential, with a vision of creating "good government" by maintaining the effectiveness of the state's administrative institutions, specifically relying on high caliber senior civil servants to set the goals and tone of the bureaucracy. Senior civil servants are expected to be of equal caliber, if not more capable than top bankers, lawyers or industrialists. The existence of a small elite group at the top of the civil service hierarchy ensures continuity of the status quo. Recruitment to the administrative service is based on highly competitive criteria, drawing primarily on applicants with top class grades in their degree programs. The Public Service Commission (PSC) issues scholarships to top students to study at domestic or overseas universities in return for eight years work in the civil service, where a rigorous performance appraisal system is applied to the administrative service (pgs. 2-4).

B.   Generalist Administration by Specialists. Many administrators have technical, scientific and other specialized educational degrees, allowing senior administrators, managers and professionals to be responsibly involved in policy decisions within their areas of specialization (pg. 4-5).

B.   Control and Accountability through various watchdog bodies, including the Auditor-General's Office, Public Accounts Committee of Parliament, and the Estimates Committee of Parliament (pg. 5-6).

C.   A Strict Anti-Corruption Emphasis throughout the public bureaucracy by enacting comprehensive legislation such as the Prevention of Corruption Act as enforced by the main anti-corruption agency, the Corrupt Practices Investigation

Bureau. In addition a policy to pay civil servants and employees of statutory boards competitive salaries and wages reduces the temptation to take bribes, or to extort and embezzle money (pg. 7).

III.   Modernization and Reforming Public Administration Procedures.

A.   Managerial and Budgetary Reform utilizes the principles and methods of business management in public administration. The Block Vote Budget Allocation Systems, Singapore Government Management Accounting System (SIGMA) provides computer-based information and analytical tools to improve the tracking and analyses of the cost of services, products or activities to gauge cost-effectiveness, measuring and evaluating the performance and results of government programs.
Performance targeting and measurement, and budgeting for results are indicators that measure cost performance, achievements or output performance (pg. 7-10).

B.   Privatization, Corporatization, Deregulation, and Divestment of statutory boards in service sectors such telecommunications, broadcasting, and public utilities serves to 1) create profit orientations, appropriate capital structures and organizational independence from bureaucratic control; and 2) provide necessary organizational autonomy and capital structures to enable new companies to invest overseas (pg. 10-12).

C.   Reform of Personnel Functions including decentralization of personnel matters; expansion of training; introduction of mixed-ranking whereby officers within different services are ranked against each other; using a dual track scheme with three benefits that, 1) increases the inflow of talent into the top management and policy making positions in the civil service; 2) opens the administrative service to new ideas and perspectives from other professions and specialists in the civil service, and; 3) enhances the career opportunities of the most capable performers (pg. 12-15).

D.   The Shift to Client-Oriented Public Administration such as community policing, enforcement of safety regulations in factories, shipyards and construction sites; food hygiene regulations in establishments, manufacturing, or food selling utilizing strict standards of industrial safety and hygiene (pg. 15). Creation of Local Administration such as town councils to manage public housing common areas, where authority was previously at higher centralized bureaucratic levels (pg. 17-18).

IV.   Adopting Administrative Reform to enhance overall socioeconomic progress; shifting to reforms based on the assumptions and principles of market; downsizing the public sector through privatization, restructure the public service to facilitate pro-market policies such as deregulation and privatization, and transformation of the public service in the image of business management by changing the nature of administrative reforms to include its focus, objectives, priorities, structures, and norms (pg. 47).

Consequences of Features are comprehensively described by Wong & Chan (pgs. 48-64) as follows:

I.   Macro-Level Changes in Administrative Reform.
Singapore is currently pursuing reforms to their public bureaucracy based on market and business management principles.   This is transforming the overall focus, objectives, priorities, and beneficiaries of the macro-level changes in their system of governmental service bureaucracy from the traditionally paternalistic "good government" model to one more reflective of corporatization, privatization and market-driven profit-orientation (pg. 48-49).

A.   Changes in the Focus of Reform has shifted from previous concern for localization to the needs of their multiethnic society to a new drive for global orientation and international interactions. This has resulted in a commensurate changes in the public services to address an expansion of their roles with foreign market forces and representatives based upon the adoption of administrative reforms developed by Western nations, such as customer-orientedness, public-private partnership, employee participation, citizen's charter, managerialism, value for money, and results-oriented management (pg. 49-50).

B.   Changes in the Objectives of Reform reflect a shift from the initial post-independence objective of nation-building and socioeconomic development to micro-economic concern for economic growth and productivity (pg. 50-51).

C.   Changes in the Priorities of Reform has shifted the direct role of the public sector in economic development to a more catalytic and indirect role, while encouraging private sector activities to actively increase in a leadership capacity toward greater privatization and downsizing (pg. 51-52).

D.   Changes in the Entitled Beneficiaries of Reform appear to emphasize more regional cooperation among members of ASEAN (Association of Southeast Asian Nations, or which Singapore was a founding member in 1985) in the areas of open markets, stabilizing commodity prices, reforming the international monetary and trading systems, and dealing with extraregional powers on trade, aid, and investment matters in an effort to foster economic gains, to decrease the trade deficit and dependence on such industrial powers as Japan and the United States (Simone, pgs. 336-337). The expectation of greater regional partnerships in improving the economic stability of the area nations' domestic situations, which will primarily benefit first the business and elite classes of their society, redefined as serving the interest of "customers" (pg. 52).

II.   Micro-Level Changes in Administrative Reform

Reforms have also had shifts in bureaucratic areas of structural trends, decision criteria, institutional patterns, and normative standards of public service programs (pg. 53).

A.   Changes in Reform in Terms of Institutional Patterns have resulted in the emergence of a new set of public sector organizations to assure political neutrality, accountability, and the integrity of the public bureaucracy and consequently to be able to carry out state policies more efficiently and effectively (pg. 53).

B.   Changes in Reform in Terms of StructuralTrends of public management, particularly in personnel matters, such as increasing bureaucratic decentralization, while maintaining some degree of central control by the appointment of board memberships by top government officials. In addition, greater opportunities for lateral entry and personnel exchange between the public and private sectors, including a program to attach Administrative Service Officers to private companies for two to three years (pg. 55).

C.   Changes in Reform in Terms of Decision Criteria has not been significant due to the meritocracy's nature of recruitment, selection, and promotion of personnel based upon the level of educational qualification, therefore the continued emphasis on the rank-in-person (qualifications) vs. the rank-in-position (based on job risks) has led to little pressure to change the decision-making paradigm.

However, due to recent emphasis on productivity and quality management in public service, and the further transition of the bureaucracy to implement the business model of management has resulted in pressures to change various aspects of performance appraisal and the compensation process and criteria (pg. 56-57).

D.   Changes in Reform in Terms of Normative Preferences is shifting from traditional public service norms such as accountability, equality, justice, neutrality, and representativeness to more market-oriented principles such as competitiveness, efficiency, productivity, and profitability (57).

III.   Implications of Changes in Administrative Reform are wide ranging both in principle, focus, and purpose. The traditional role of the public bureaucracy has been to enhance socioeconomic development as a means of the government to improve the quality of life, reduce poverty, enhance social development and stability, and decrease inter-ethnic income disparities. Consequently, the public sector had played crucial roles in providing for the needs of education, employment, health, and housing. However, the current market-orientation and emphasis that has resulted in a declining focus on indigenous concerns in preference to international market demands has also lessened the public service's authority, control, monitoring, and delivery of infrastructure services to average citizens, resulting in a new emphasis on serving the needs of elite "customers". These changes may create more opportunities for corruption due to the blurring of the lines of moral responsibility in the arena of profit making as a primary service criteria while potentially transforming public servants traditionally devoted to public concerns to that of serving business interests and priorities instead. The ethical dilemma and identity confusion that market-emphasis creates within the public bureaucracy (pg. 58-61).

A paradox appears to lie at the heart of the interplay between individuality and social stability within a context of a paternalistic polity undergoing transformation and public bureaucracy that attempts to moderate individual behavior through a behaviorist system of rewards and punishment. On the one hand, there's a tendency to reject sociological explanations of social order altogether, thus to conceptualize the phenomenon purely in terms of individual choices made through the exercise of free agency. On the other hand, laws and practices such as certain forms of censorship and the intolerance shown in meting out punishment promotes the notion that particular social conditions and factors have causal linkage to certain types of individual behavior.

Consequently, there exists in Singapore a high degree of faith in the capacity of laws and administrative measures to affect individual behavior, as exemplified by incentives and disincentives relating to various social behaviors, and laws regulating spitting and the toilet flushing (Perera). The emphasis on social order is viewed as the foundation of economic progress, but in the opinion of some political observers, legislated civility in Singapore exceeds the primary purpose of order.

This suggests that the move towards recognizing some universally relevant principles about human rights, crime and other social issues does not represent a decisive shift in orientation on the part of the establishment government. Mainstream opinion generally approve these principles, but it may only be a process by which elites are seeking more philosophical justification for defending their privileged socioeconomic status. The government primarily remains a monolithic entity; however, market and business-based reforms are decentralizing control into increased bureaucratic and corporatized consensus building, one that reflects the majority or dominant view within the business community.

Government and senior civil service circles recognize that consensus is the outcome of a process of interaction (although on unequal terms) between the mainstream and non-elite groups, such as the working class and the liberal-inclined intelligentsia; however, it's unclear to what extent the government perceives the need to engage more actively with non-elite groups in order to preserve its dominant political position (Perera). The current trend toward global and international emphasis and customer-orientation suggests increased possibilities that market-orientation offers the elitist private sectors greater opportunities to successfully organize and pursue their own agendas, to the potential detriment of the general public. Consequently government consensus on individual rights and other issues depends on the success with which non-elite groups are able to express and promote their own agendas in competition with the growing emphasis of the pubic bureaucracy to prioritize services foremost to "customers" who are able to pay for it. Singapore's program to relax centralized control is emulating the Western capitalistic model.

A bit of anecdotal information updating the life of Michael Fay at age 22. He was arrested in Florida on drug charges by a deputy responding to neighbors' complaints about loud music only four years after he received four strikes of the cane in Singapore. Fay, a college student was charged with possession of drug paraphernalia and less than 20 grams of marijuana (AP). In Singapore, possession of a larger amount of marijuana or a smaller amount of other illegal drugs would have made him eligible for the death penalty, which is applied to several crimes including murder, discharge of a firearm in the commission of a crime (whether or not anyone is killed), illegal arms possession (3 or more weapons), drug trafficking, and illegal arms dealing among others. The Singaporean bureaucracy metes out these types of social policies as both punishment and deterrence to intimidate the populace to normative social order and responsible individual behavior, as the societal stability required for continued economic progress.

References

Associated Press (AP). *Singapore Caning Victim Arrested.* Winter Park, Florida. April 2, 1998. http://silcon.com/~ptave/n-b24.htm (4/4/01).

Lee, Kuan Yew, James R. Gaines, Joelle Attinger, William Dowell and Sandra Burton. *A Rigorous Case for Morality; Singapore's Lee Kuan Yew Speaks Out On Caning.* TIME Domestic. May 9, 1994. Volume 143, No. 19. http://www.time.com/time/magazine/archive/1994/940509/940509.interview.html (4/4/01).

Perera, Leon. *The Michael Fay Controversy - What Was At Stake?* The Straits Times, October 12, 1993, Forum, page 2. http://www.happening.com.sg/commentary/michaelfay.html (4/4/01).

Simone, Vera. *The Asian Pacific Political and Economic Development in a Global Context.* New York, NY: Addison Wesley Longman, Inc. (2001).

Wong, Hoi-kwok, and Hon S. Chan (editors). *Handbook of Comparative Public Administration in the Asia-Pacific Basin.* New York, NY: Marcel Dekker, Inc. (1999).

---

13 - <u>Conclusions</u>

Men are genetically violent, and when coupled by cultural rules that have generally been created by men to justify their aggressiveness and dominance over women, it's understandable why traumatic criminal acts such as rape and violence against women is pandemic, particularly here in America that has one of the highest violent crime rates among developed nations.

Is the solution to have government and the legal system to model itself after one of the most crime free and peaceful nations on earth that has also attained an educational level and real purchasing power that exceeds that in America? We may have much to learn from their political and social structure, however, the U.S. was a nation founded in violence. Our culture celebrates violence as the final solution to conflict, whether on the international stage of warfare or in personal relations. It is highly unlikely the American populace would sheepishly go along with excessive government control of their "freedoms."

The real solutions to aggressiveness in men and the tendency of certain men to rape and kill are comprehensive and involve almost all aspects of what make boys into men. It is highly unlikely those culturally inculcated values can be changed

except over generations if all of the proposed solutions were to be simultaneously supported and implemented. But steps must be taken to gradually change our culture of the widespread sexual exploitation of females that contribute to attitudes by certain men with out of control sexual and violent urges that raping and killing women is okay. Anything less is unacceptable for a nation that is supposedly the torch for freedom in the world.

Of course the courts have removed justice as one of the anti-crime pillars in society. Men who rape then kills their female victims languish forever on "Death Row" with most never seeing their execution date. Taxpayers waste their hard earned money supporting these rapists and murderers who become hardened criminals during their stay in the penitentiaries, taking away needed funds from our children, infrastructure, and public services. The penal system is no longer a deterrent to rapists and murderers, and the "Three Strikes Law" has convinced rapists that it's better to kill the victims, than to suffer their third strike and be incarcerated for life. With murdering the victim, there's a good chance they won't ever get caught.

Perhaps it's time for our justice system to focus on giving the families of the victims some real justice, instead of calling effective penalties and deterrents as "cruel and unusual punishment". The penalty for rape should be physical castration, and every murderer deserves swift and decisive justice... execution. The most humane form of execution has already been invented hundreds of years ago... the guillotine. Guarantee rapists their penalty will be life in prison plus castration, and murderers get their heads lopped off into a bucket within five years of conviction, and it's certain the rate of rape and murder will fall drastically.

An eye for an eye and a tooth for a tooth is real justice.

Author's Note:

References

Blair-Loy, Mary, 1999. "Career patterns of executive women in finance: all optimal matching analysis." American Journal of Sociology, Vol. 104, Issue 5 (Mar., 1999), 1346-1397. Retrieved from the World Wide Web, March 1, 2002 from http://www.jstor.org.

Freese, Jeremy, and Brian Powell, 1999. "Sociobiology, status, and parental investment in sons and daughters: testing the Trivers-Willard Hypothesis." *American Journal of Sociology*, Vol. 104, Issue 6 (May, 1999), 1704-1743. Retrieved from the World Wide Web, March 1, 2002 from http://www.jstor.org.

Han, Shin Kap, and Phyllis Moen, 1999. "Clocking out: temporal patterning of retirement." *American Journal of Sociology*, Vol. 105, Issue 1 (July, 1999), 229-236. Retrieved from the World Wide Web, March 1, 2002 from http://www.jstor.org.

Manza, Jeff, and Clem Brooks, 1998. " The gender gap in U.S. presidential elections; when, why? implications?" *American Journal of Sociology*, Vol. 103, Issue 5 (Mar., 1998), 1235-1266. Retrieved from the World Wide Web, March 1, 2002 from http://www.jstor.org.

www.ingramcontent.com/pod-product-compliance
Lightning Source LLC
Chambersburg PA
CBHW070202290526
45789CB00002B/872